VIDEO SCRIPT 1

Episodes 1-12

Boston, Massachusetts   Burr Ridge, Illinois   Dubuque, Iowa   Madison, Wisconsin
New York, New York   San Francisco, California   St. Louis, Missouri
Bangkok   Bogotá   Caracas   Lisbon   London   Madrid   Mexico City
Milan   New Delhi   Seoul   Singapore   Sydney   Taipei   Toronto

McGraw-Hill

A Division of The **McGraw·Hill** *Companies*

CONNECT WITH ENGLISH: VIDEO SCRIPT 1

domestic   2 3 4 5 6 7 8 9 0 COU COU 9 0 0 9 8
international   2 3 4 5 6 7 8 9 0 COU COU 9 0 0 9 8

ISBN 0-07-365873-1

Editorial director: Thalia Dorwick
Publisher: Tim Stookesberry
Development editor: Pam Tiberia
Marketing manager: Tracy Landrum
Production supervisor: Richard DeVitto
Print materials consultant: Marilyn Rosenthal
Project manager: Shannon McIntyre, Function Thru Form, Inc.
Design and Electronic Production: Function Thru Form, Inc.
Typeface: Frutiger
Printer and Binder: Courier Corp.

Library of Congress Catalog Card No.: 97-75579

http://www.mhhe.com

EPISODE

1

Rebecca's Dream

PART 1

1 *ON THE STREET, OUTSIDE A HOTEL—NIGHT*

2 *We are in Boston, outside of a hotel. Matt and Rebecca are talking. Matt's truck is outside of the hotel.*
3 *Rebecca opens her door. So does Matt. They are arguing.*

4 **REBECCA** No!

5 **MATT** Yes!

6 **REBECCA** You're wrong.

7 **MATT** I'm right and you know it.

8 **REBECCA** Look, I have to go.

9 **MATT** Rebecca, we have to talk.

10 **REBECCA** Not now, Matt.

11 **MATT** I'll wait right here 'til you're done.

12 **REBECCA** Matt, you don't have to wait for me.

13 **MATT** Yes, I do. I'll be right here.

14 **REBECCA** It'll be a couple of hours.

15 *Matt shrugs his shoulders. He is going to wait for Rebecca.*

16 **MATT** All right. Bye.

17 *Rebecca walks across the street toward the back of the building. Matt yells out after her.*

18 **MATT** Where are you going? The front door is over there.

19 **REBECCA** I have to use the employee's entrance.

20 *Rebecca disappears. Matt shakes his head.*

21 *HOTEL KITCHEN*

22 *Rebecca is in a kitchen. She sees a waiter and asks him for directions.*

23 **REBECCA** Excuse me, the Gold Room? This way? Thanks. (*The waiter points.*)

24 *Rebecca enters a fancy conference room where she meets Steve, her music partner. He is setting up his*
25 *music.*

26 *THE GOLD ROOM*

27 **REBECCA** Hi, Steve.

28 **STEVE** Hello, Rebecca. We're almost ready.

29 **REBECCA** Listen, I need to change.

30 **STEVE** There's a ladies' room over there. (*Rebecca rushes off to change.*)

31 **REBECCA** I'll be right back.

32 *Rebecca stops and says hello to Steve's pregnant wife.*

33 **REBECCA** Hi, Jessica.

34 **JESSICA** How are you?

35 **REBECCA** Good.

36 *Rebecca goes to the ladies' room to put on her singing clothes and makeup. Hotel guests begin to come into*
37 *the Gold Room. Steve begins to play his piano. Nobody pays much attention. Back in the ladies' room,*
38 *Rebecca fixes her hair and puts on lipstick. She looks very nice when she returns to the stage area.*
39 *Then Rebecca and Steve get ready to play on a small stage.*

40 **REBECCA** Hello, Hello.

41 *No one pays much attention to her.*

42 **REBECCA** Welcome to the Gold Room. I'm Rebecca Casey and this is Steve Davis.

43 *Again, no one pays attention.*

44 **REBECCA** Here's a song I wrote. I call it 'Traveling Light.'

45 *She sings her song and she is good. The people at the hotel are busy. They talk about their business and don't*
46 *really listen to the music. The music stops when a waiter drops some dishes.*

47 *THE GOLD ROOM—LATER THAT SAME NIGHT*

48 *The Gold Room is now empty. Only Steve, who is packing up his piano music, and his pregnant wife are*
49 *left. A conference manager comes in and gives him an envelope. It is their pay. Rebecca comes back and she*
50 *is wearing her regular clothes.*

51 **STEVE** (*to wife*) Why don't you wait out in the lobby. (*Steve's wife leaves.*) (*to Rebecca*)
52   Here's your share. Twenty . . . thirty . . . forty . . . and five.

53 **REBECCA** Forty-five. Good thing I have a day job.

54 **STEVE** Good thing we both do. (*He shakes his head.*)

55 **REBECCA** We'll do better next time.

56 **STEVE** Rebecca, I have something to tell you. There isn't going to be a next time,
57   for me.

58 **REBECCA** What?

59 **STEVE** I'm tired of this. My wife's expecting. The bills are piling up. This (*waving the cash*)
60   isn't a salary. It's peanuts.

61 **REBECCA** But, Steve, we're getting lots of calls . . . We're playing at a wedding next week . . .

62 **STEVE** I want to spend my weekends with my wife, not at weddings for people I don't
63   know.

64 **REBECCA** Steve, you shouldn't, we've worked so hard.

65 **STEVE** (*interrupting*) You know how I feel . . . It's always the same old story: no money, no
66   appreciation. Sorry, Rebecca, but this is it for me. You'll find another piano
67   player. Bye. Take care of yourself.

68 *Steve walks away. Rebecca looks very sad—as if she just lost a good friend.*

PART 2

69 *OUTSIDE THE HOTEL—NIGHT*

70 *Matt is waiting for Rebecca. She's very quiet.*

71 **MATT**   So, you're mad I waited, right?

72 **REBECCA** No, I'm not angry.

73 **MATT**   So, what's wrong?

74 **REBECCA** Steve says he can't take it anymore.

75 **MATT**   He's quitting? (*Rebecca nods "yes" in answer to Matt's question.*) Maybe he's got the
76   right idea.

77 **REBECCA** Look, I'm not quitting. I have to find another partner.

78 **MATT**   Rebecca, you're banging your head against the wall. You're never gonna make it
79   in the music business. It's too tough.

80 **REBECCA** Why are you so negative?

81 **MATT**   I'm realistic.

82 **REBECCA** Look, Matt, success takes time. I'm going to make it. That's why I'm going to
83   music school.

84 **MATT**   Music school . . . What am I going to do while you're in music school?

85 *Rebecca doesn't answer. She stays silent.*

86 **MATT**   We had a relationship, you know?

87 **REBECCA** We still do.

88 **MATT**   What's happening to us? You have two jobs; I have two jobs. You have to take
89   care of your father. There's no time.

90 **REBECCA** I'm sorry, Matt . . . It's hard to find time.

91 **MATT**   A real relationship takes time, you know?

92 **REBECCA** I know . . . It's late. I have to be up early for work tomorrow.

93 **MATT**   All right, I'll take you home.

94 *FRONT ENTRANCE OF THE CASEY APARTMENT*

95 *Matt's car pulls up. They are saying goodnight.*

96 **MATT**   So, about our date on Thursday . . . ? I'll pick you up at seven, OK?

97 **REBECCA** Sounds good. (*He gives her a kiss. There is still some feeling between them.*)

98 **MATT**   This is really crazy, Rebecca Casey.

99 **REBECCA** Good night, Matt.

PART 3

100 *CASEY APARTMENT—NIGHT*

101 *Rebecca enters a simple middle-class apartment. She sees the mail on the front-hall table. She sees a large*
102 *package and finds that it's from the Boston School of Music. She is happy to see it. She picks it up and*
103 *hurries off to her room.*

104 **REBECCA** Oh, good. It's here.

105 *REBECCA'S BEDROOM*

106 *Rebecca enters her bedroom and opens the package. While she is reading the brochure, we see a number of*
107 *pictures from Rebecca's life. On the mirror there are photos that tell the story of Rebecca's life. We see a*
108 *photo of Rebecca, her dad, and her brother. We see a large photo of Rebecca in a baseball uniform. Rebecca*
109 *is happy and smiling here. She is a basball player. We see a photo of Rebecca's mother as a young woman*
110 *and a photo of Rebecca as a little girl. Rebecca looks like her mother. Rebecca takes a videotape out of its*
111 *case. She gets up and leaves the bedroom with the tape.*

112 *FRONT ROOM*

113 *Rebecca puts the tape into the VCR. She turns on the TV and begins the tape. Rebecca is watching the tape*
114 *about the school. She is getting very excited about what she sees. This is the happiest she has been in a long time.*

115 *SCENES FROM BOSTON SCHOOL OF MUSIC TAPE*

116 *This tape is like a commercial. It shows professors talking about the school, and it shows musical*
117 *performances by the students.*

118 *DIALOGUE FROM THE TAPE*

119 **NARRATOR—PROMO TAPE**
120   Welcome to the Boston School of Music, where your musical career begins.

121 **STUDENT—BOSTON SCHOOL OF MUSIC**
122   The Boston School of Music has given me everything that I wanted in a school.
123   The Boston School of Music has just been my home. And, because of that
124   foundation, I'm able to be what I want to be.

125 *INSIDE THE FRONT ROOM*

126 *As Rebecca is watching the tape, another door opens slowly. Her brother, Kevin, a seventeen-year-old senior*
127 *in high school, is standing there. The noise from the tape woke him up.*

128 **KEVIN**   What's goin' on, Beck?

129 **REBECCA** Sorry. Is it too loud?

130 **KEVIN**   A little. Turn it down so you don't wake up Dad.

131 *She turns the volume down and sits closer to the TV. He sits on the sofa, half asleep.*

132 *DIALOGUE FROM THE TAPE*

133 **TEACHER** The faculty is very high quality, and I think students have some wonderful
134   opportunities.

135 *Kevin begins to talk to Rebecca again.*

136 **KEVIN**   So, are you going to this school?

137 **REBECCA** Yeah . . . if I get accepted. I'm applying to other colleges, but this is my first
138   choice.

139 **KEVIN**   Hey, they're pretty good.

140 **REBECCA** Yeah, this school's one of the best . . .

141 DIALOGUE FROM THE TAPE
142 **NARRATOR—PROMO TAPE**
143   Make your dreams come true at the Boston School of Music. Apply now!

EPISODE 2

Differences

PART 1

1 CASEY APARTMENT—NIGHT

2 *Kevin is sitting at the kitchen table. He is separating cookies into two halves and eating them. Rebecca enters*
3 *carrying the brochure.*

4 REBECCA Kevin, I can write my songs on a computer. They have a computer lab . . . It
5   opens up the possibilities of song composition . . .

6 *Kevin looks inside the refrigerator. He's not really listening to Rebecca, but hears the word "possibility."*

7 KEVIN   What's the possibility of getting some food in this house soon?

8 REBECCA I'm going grocery shopping tomorrow. Put what you want on the list.

9 *Kevin pulls the list off the refrigerator. Rebecca is now filling out the forms from the school.*

10 REBECCA I can't believe how many forms I have to fill out.

11 *Kevin shows Rebecca an empty box of cereal.*

12 KEVIN   I can't believe we're out of cereal.

13 REBECCA Put it on the list.

14 *Rebecca begins to fill out an application form. She writes her name on the form.*

15 REBECCA *(writing)* Name: Rebecca Casey
16   Address: 1097 E Street, Apt. #3
17   Boston, MA 02168

18 *Kevin takes a peanut butter jar out of the cupboard and opens it.*

19 KEVIN   We're almost out of peanut butter . . .

20 REBECCA I just bought that jar.

21 KEVIN   Hey, look, a coupon . . . two for the price of one . . . I know, put it on the list.

22 *Rebecca continues with the form she is filling out. Now the two of them, brother and sister, are writing at*
23 *the table.*

24 REBECCA *(filling in the form)* Phone number: (617) 686-7731
25   Age: 28
26   Father: Patrick Casey
27   Mother: Margaret Casey (deceased)

28 *Kevin is eating cookies and peanut butter.*

29 KEVIN   We should get more cookies.

30	REBECCA	Gee, they want to know everything—my interests, hobbies, sports, awards, on
31		and on . . . I'll be here all night.
32	KEVIN	Do you think this college thing is a good idea?
33	REBECCA	Yeah, for me it is. It's the only way I'm going to get anywhere in the music world.

34 *Kevin digs a cookie into the peanut butter.*

35	REBECCA	When are you going to give up junk food and eat something healthy?
36	KEVIN	When healthy food tastes as good as cookies and peanut butter.
37	REBECCA	*(laughing)* Oh, good night.

38 *REBECCA'S BEDROOM*

39 *Rebecca is in her nightgown and she is sitting in front of her mirror. She is looking at a photo of her mother*
40 *on the dresser.*

| 41 | REBECCA | I hope I can make it, Mom. |

42 *Rebecca turns off the light and goes to bed.*

43 *CASEY APARTMENT—MORNING*

44 *Rebecca is fixing a lunch and puts it into the refrigerator. Kevin runs in, goes to the refrigerator, drinks from*
45 *a carton of milk, and puts it back. He is dressed in a jacket and tie, shorts, and sneakers.*

46	KEVIN	I am late for school.
47	REBECCA	Don't drink from the carton!
48	KEVIN	Milk tastes better this way.
49	REBECCA	You drive me insane. Why are you wearing shorts and a tie?
50	KEVIN	High school graduation pictures.
51	REBECCA	What do you mean? *(Kevin demonstrates for Rebecca.)*
52	KEVIN	Graduation pictures . . . you know. They take the picture from here up. They
53		don't take a picture of your legs.
54	REBECCA	Are all your exams finished?
55	KEVIN	I just have my math final.
56	REBECCA	*(concerned)* Kevin.
57	KEVIN	Beck, don't worry. Math is a breeze. I've got to go.

58 *Kevin grabs his books from a table and heads toward the front door. His father comes out of the bathroom in*
59 *robe and pajamas. He walks with a limp and uses a cane.*

| 60 | KEVIN | Hi, Dad. Bye, Dad. |
| 61 | DAD | Don't slam the door! . . .Thanks. |

62 *Kevin leaves, slamming the door behind him. Dad, grumpy this morning, limps into the kitchen.*
63 *Dad comes in and finds a cup of coffee on the table. He picks it up and drinks it.*

| 64 | REBECCA | Hi, Dad. Why are you up so early? *(Dad shrugs.)* Where's my coffee? |
| 65 | DAD | What, this? Is this yours? I'm sorry. |

66	REBECCA	That's OK. I'm late anyway. I'll get coffee at work.
67		*She picks up an envelope that is on the table.*
68	DAD	What's that?
69	REBECCA	It's my application to the Boston School of Music. I have to mail it today.
70	DAD	*(not really happy)* Oh. Not another school application.
71 72	REBECCA	Yes, another school application . . . By the way, does Kevin ever tell you how his final exams are going?
73	DAD	No, he doesn't tell me anything . . . I try to talk to him but . . .
74 75	REBECCA	He has a final today. I don't even know if he studied for it. He won't graduate if he doesn't pass his exams.
76	DAD	I'll talk to him.
77	REBECCA	I have to go! Your lunch is in the fridge. *(She starts to leave.)*
78	DAD	Do you have enough change for the bus?
79	REBECCA	Yes, I have some, thanks.
80 81	DAD	Becky . . . don't slam the door. *(She closes it gently.)* Thanks. *(He feels a sharp pain and then it passes. He continues to drink his coffee.)*

PART 2

82 *FACTORY, WORK AREA—MORNING*

83 *Sandy is leaning over a computer board. She is wearing safety glasses. Rebecca sits down.*

84	REBECCA	Sandy.
85	SANDY	Hey, girl. You just made it. Is everything OK?
86	REBECCA	Yeah, I was up late last night.
87	SANDY	With Matt?
88	REBECCA	No, with this. Look . . .

89 *Sandy looks up. Rebecca shows her a brochure from the Boston School of Music.*

90	SANDY	What is it?
91 92	REBECCA	It's a brochure from the Boston School of Music. I sent my application in this morning.
93	SANDY	Good for you! This place looks expensive.
94	REBECCA	It is. But it'll be worth it . . . if I get accepted.
95	SANDY	And if you don't get in?
96	REBECCA	I've got my backup schools . . . maybe I'll get into one of them.
97	SANDY	How many colleges are you applying to?
98	REBECCA	Four . . .
99	SANDY	Four? Why so many? That's a lot of work.
100 101	REBECCA	And a lot of money, just to apply . . . But I've been dreaming of this for a long time.

102	**SANDY**	Your dreams are so . . . big, exciting. I mean, my dreams are real simple—get
103		married, have a family, stuff like that.
104	**REBECCA**	I don't know, I can't explain it . . . I just want to know everything I can about
105		music. I'll get my degree and make something of myself.
106	**SANDY**	Well, when you become a big star and you get your first hit song, don't forget
107		your friends here at the factory.
108	**REBECCA**	Me? Forget? Never. I'll even send you a free copy.
109	**SANDY**	You're all heart.

PART 3

110 CASEY APARTMENT, FRONT ROOM—AFTERNOON

111 *A tape from the Boston School of Music is playing. Dad reaches over and shuts it off. The door opens and*
112 *Kevin enters carrying a big box.*

113	**KEVIN**	Hello! Dad!
114	**DAD**	You're home early.
115	**KEVIN**	It was a half day, today.
116	**DAD**	How come?
117	**KEVIN**	I just had one final and graduation pictures.
118	**DAD**	What's that? (*Kevin begins to open the box.*)
119	**KEVIN**	My cap and gown. (*Kevin holds up each as he describes it. Then he slips on the gown.*)
120		Let me show you. It smells funny! And, the cap . . . How about it—Kevin Casey,
121		high school graduate. (*Kevin looks at himself in the mirror, quite pleased with his*
122		*appearance.*)
123	**DAD**	It's too bad your mother can't see you now . . .
124	**KEVIN**	What's for lunch?
125	**DAD**	Kevin, come sit here. (*Kevin sits on the couch.*) Rebecca and I are both worried
126		about your finals. How was your exam today?
127	**KEVIN**	A breeze. Math's my best subject. It was an easy test.
128	**DAD**	Well, good . . . What about the others—science, history? . . .
129	**KEVIN**	Dad, give me a break! I'll pass them all with flying colors.

130 *FACTORY—AFTERNOON*

131 *A person hands Rebecca and Sandy their paychecks. They open them.*

132	**REBECCA**	Oh, thanks.
133	**SANDY**	This won't even cover my bills.
134	**REBECCA**	Your whole paycheck?
135	**SANDY**	Yeah. I lent some money to Jack.
136	**REBECCA**	You can sure kiss that money goodbye.
137	**SANDY**	Why are you so hard on Jack? You know, he's really a good guy.
138	**REBECCA**	I'm sorry, I just don't think that . . . Let's forget it.

139 *BANK*

140 *Sandy and Rebecca are cashing their checks.*

141 **SANDY**   I'd like to cash this check, please.

142 **TELLER**   Do you have an account at this bank?

143 **SANDY**   Yes.

144 **TELLER**   Can I see some form of identification, please?

145 *Sandy hands him her driver's license. Sandy turns to Rebecca and says impatiently*

146 **SANDY**   Why do I always have to show my I.D.?

147 **REBECCA**   (*whispering*) He's a new teller. Hey, they do it for your protection.

148 **SANDY**   Right, so we have to show our I.D. every single time. (*The teller counts out Sandy's*
149   *money.*)

150 **TELLER**   Twenty, forty, sixty, eighty, a hundred, a hundred and twenty, hundred and forty,
151   hundred and sixty, hundred and eighty, two hundred.

152 **SANDY**   Thanks.

153 *Rebecca steps up to the teller. She hands him a deposit slip, her check, and her passbook.*

154 **REBECCA**   Hi, I'd like to deposit the whole check into my savings account, please.

155 *Sandy is counting her money to make sure it's all there.*

156 **SANDY**   How can you live without cash?

157 **REBECCA**   I get money from the cash machine . . . forty dollars at a time.

158 **SANDY**   I can't stand you, Rebecca.

159 *ATM MACHINE*

160 *Rebecca is using her cash card to get forty dollars from the machine.*

161 **SANDY**   Don't they charge for these cash machines?

162 **REBECCA**   It depends on what kind of account you have, and whether you have enough
163   money in it.

164 **SANDY**   And you have that much money saved?

165 **REBECCA**   How else am I going to pay for college? Save, save, save.

166 *She gets her money, cash card, and a receipt.*

167 **SANDY**   Wow.

168 *CASEY APARTMENT—AFTERNOON*

169 **DAD**   Do you know about this videotape?

170 **KEVIN**   The Boston School of Music? Yeah, this is the music school that Becky wants to
171   go to.

172 **DAD**   Why doesn't she study something practical, like business? She'll never make any
173   money with a degree in music.

174 **KEVIN**   You never know.

A Visit to the Doctor

PART 1

1 *HOSPITAL OUT-PATIENT CLINIC—MORNING*

2 *Dad and Rebecca stand at the receptionist's desk.*

3 **RECEPTIONIST** May I help you?

4 **DAD**　　　　I have a ten o'clock appointment with Dr. Samji. The name's Patrick Casey.

5 **RECEPTIONIST** *(She enters the name in the computer.)* Could you spell that for me?

6 **DAD**　　　　C-A-S-E-Y.

7 **RECEPTIONIST** Yes. Please have a seat, and we'll call you.

8 *Rebecca and Dad walk slowly over to a bench and sit. Dad is in pain and Rebecca gives him a questioning*
9 *look.*

10 **DAD**　　　　My leg's stiff today.

11 **REBECCA** Be sure to ask the doctor if there's anything you can do about it.

12 **DAD**　　　　They never have anything useful to say to me.

13 **REBECCA** That's not true. And if you don't take care of your leg, it's only going to get
14 　　　　　worse.

15 **REBECCA** They say exercise can help, you know.

16 **DAD**　　　　OK, OK.

17 **REBECCA** You're in a bad mood today.

18 **DAD**　　　　Well, I'm doing the best I can. Hospitals make me nervous . . . Doctors put me on
19 　　　　　edge . . . And I'm worried about my kids. One says she wants to go to music
20 　　　　　school . . .

21 **REBECCA** So . . .?

22 **DAD**　　　　But music? What kind of a job will you get if you study music?

23 **REBECCA** Come on, Dad . . . Music is big business. There are all kinds of jobs.

24 **DAD**　　　　Sure, turning pages for some dumb piano player . . .

25 **REBECCA** Come on. You know my dream is to be a songwriter.

26 **DAD**　　　　You and a million others.

27 **REBECCA** I think I have some talent.

28 **DAD**　　　　Why don't you study nursing or something?

29 **REBECCA** It's not me. It's not what I want. I want to study music.

30 **DAD**　　　　Well, if you ask me . . . I think you're making a big mistake.

31 **REBECCA** Not if it's what I want to do.

32 **RECEPTIONIST** Mr. Casey.

33 **DAD**   You're a stubborn woman.

34 **REBECCA**   *(smiling)* You bet! I take after my father.

PART 2

35 *HOSPITAL EXAMINING ROOM*

36 *Dr. Samji is examining Mr. Casey. He examines his eyes, heart, and blood pressure.*

37 **DR. SAMJI** Look left, right, up, down. What happened to your leg, Mr. Casey?

38 **DAD**   Oh, a wall fell on it.

39 **DR. SAMJI** A wall?

40 **DAD**   Yeah, when I was a fireman, I was in a hotel fire . . .

41 *FLASHBACK OF FIRE SCENE*

42 *We see scenes from the fire where Mr. Casey had his accident. There is fire and smoke everywhere.*

43 *HOSPITAL EXAMINING ROOM*

44 **DAD**   . . . I've been on disability pay ever since the accident.

45 *A nurse enters with an X-ray. Dr. Samji studies the test results.*

46 **DR. SAMJI** Let's have a little talk here, Mr. Casey. We have found several potential problems.
47 Your cholesterol is very high, the EKG tells us there is a slight heart problem, and
48 the circulation in your leg is . . . ah, how should I put it . . . getting worse. If we
49 don't do something right away, your current situation could lead to a stroke or
50 heart attack . . . We strongly recommend that you start an exercise program. And
51 we have to put you on a strict diet. And get this prescription filled . . .

52 **DAD**   Whatever you say, Doc.

53 *OUTSIDE THE HOSPITAL*

54 *Rebecca and her father wait for a taxi. Her father's very quiet.*

55 **REBECCA**   Here comes a taxi. So, what did the doctor say?

56 **DAD**   Not much. Everything's OK. No real problems.

57 *The taxi arrives and Rebecca opens the door for her father. He struggles to get into the cab. He is in pain as*
58 *he gets into the car.*

59 **REBECCA**   Do you need to stop at the drugstore?

60 **DAD**   No. Later maybe. Let's go straight home.

61 *INSIDE THE CASEY APARTMENT—LATE AFTERNOON*

62 *Rebecca's dressed and ready to go out. The buzzer rings. She says goodnight to her father. Mr. Casey is*
63 *eating junk food and watching television.*

64 **DAD**   Becky. Buzzer.

65 *She goes to the door and speaks into the intercom.*

66 **REBECCA**   I'll be right down, Matt. *(to Dad)* I won't be late. Can I get you anything before
67 I leave?

68 **DAD**   No, no. I'll be fine.

69 *She gives him a kiss.*

70 **DAD**   What's that for?

71 **REBECCA**   Because I love you.

72 **DAD**   I love you, too, honey.

73 *Rebecca gives him a hug. He's embarrassed by it and makes a fuss.*

74 **DAD**   Go on. Matt's waiting.

75 **REBECCA**   See you later.

76 *She leaves with a box of cookies. Dad sits alone—a tired, old man afraid of what he knows.*

PART 3

77 *BACKYARD PARTY—EARLY EVENING*

78 *The party is a typical Memorial Day barbecue. There are lights and there is a barbecue grill filled with*
79 *hamburgers, hot dogs, and sausages. There is typical party food such as beer, soft drinks, and chips. Friends*
80 *and couples have gathered together on this cool evening. The host of the party is Sal, who is wearing a funny*
81 *apron. Rebecca and Matt arrive at the barbecue. Rebecca gives Sal a box of cookies from a bakery.*

82 **SAL**   Hey, welcome to our fourth annual Memorial Day cookout. Coming up, one of
83   my famous charcoal-broiled hamburgers . . . and how 'bout an all-American hot
84   dog . . . and, of course, Sal's homemade Boston baked beans.

85 **DOROTHY**   So, how have you been?

86 **REBECCA**   Oh, so busy, you know, with my day job, and some gigs at night, guitar
87   lessons, and . . .

88 **DOROTHY**   Are you still working at the factory?

89 **REBECCA**   I'm hoping to go to college . . . music school.

90 **DOROTHY**   *(surprised)* Good for you. Which one?

91 **REBECCA**   Well, my first choice is the Boston School of Music, but I've applied to four
92   colleges, all together.

93 **DOROTHY**   Oh, all four will want you, I mean you have such a great voice! I wish I had a
94   talent like that.

95 **REBECCA**   Come on, you have a husband who loves you, a beautiful daughter, and your own
96   apartment . . . I mean, what more could you . . .

97 **DOROTHY**   You're right. I mean . . . I can't complain. Life is good. So, what does Matt think
98   about your plans to study music?

99 **REBECCA**   He doesn't really understand. He doesn't think I'll make it.

100 **DOROTHY** Men. They're all alike. All they think about is money . . . . and sex.

101 **REBECCA** Yeah . . .

102 *Sandy and Jack arrive. It is clear that Jack has been drinking.*

103 **JACK**   Sal . . .

104 **SAL**   How ya doin'?

105	JACK	I'm excellent. How ya doin'? Good to see ya.
106	SAL	Nice to see ya.
107	JACK	Feeling good? . . . Hey, Rebecca, you get more lovely every day . . . Look at you!

108 *He gives Rebecca a big hug.*

| 109 | REBECCA | *(pushing away)* Thanks, Jack . . . |
| 110 | JACK | Hey, but Sandy, she's the love of my life. |

111 *Sandy is embarrassed by Jack.*

112	SANDY	Jack . . .
113	JACK	*(to Sandy)* Hey, I'm thirsty. I'm going to get a drink. You want anything?
114	SANDY	No, maybe later. Thanks.

115 *Jack leaves to get himself a beer and then walks over to the volleyball game.*

116	REBECCA	Jack's in a good mood!
117	SANDY	No, not really. He's had too many beers. He lost his job yesterday.
118	REBECCA	Oh, no . . .

119 *At the barbecue some people are playing volleyball. A little girl runs to a table to get a cookie.*

120	SANDY	*(to Rebecca)* She is so cute. I want to have a little girl like that some day.
121	REBECCA	Last time I checked, you need a man for that . . . the right man . . .
122	SANDY	I know.
123	REBECCA	. . . someone who will be a good father.
124	SANDY	It's hard to imagine Jack as a Dad. He gets so crazy sometimes . . .

125 *Jack is playing volleyball with the other guys. He's at the net. A player on the opposite team slams the ball*
126 *back at him and hits his elbow. Jack gets angry and leaves the game. He comes up to Sandy.*

127	JACK	Babe, I'm leaving.
128	SANDY	We just got here.
129	JACK	So?
130	SANDY	I haven't even said hello to Sal.
131	JACK	I'm leaving. If you want to stay, you can stay. I'm leaving. OK. Is that OK? Excuse
132		me, Rebecca.

133 *Jack turns and leaves. Sandy, uncertain what to do, finally turns to Rebecca and says:*

134	SANDY	Tell Sal something came up.
135	REBECCA	What was it? The volleyball game?
136	SANDY	No, just tell him the truth: Jack's upset because he lost his job.

137 *Rebecca watches with great sadness as her friend leaves. Sal appears behind her.*

| 138 | SAL | What's with him? Did he lose his temper again? |
| 139 | REBECCA | Yeah. And he lost his job, too. Poor Sandy. |

EPISODE
4
Celebrations

PART 1

1 *HIGH SCHOOL GRADUATION—DAY*

2 *Dad, Rebecca, and Aunt Molly are sitting together.*

3 **AUNT MOLLY** Where's Kevin? I don't see him.

4 **REBECCA** He's in the second row, Aunt Molly. (*Graduation music is playing.*)

5 **PRINCIPAL** Will the Graduating Class of Boston Latin High School, please come forward
6   and receive your diplomas?

7 *The principal reads the names of students. Kevin and other students receive their diplomas. Dad, Rebecca,*
8 *and Aunt Molly look very proud of Kevin.*

9 **AUNT MOLLY** . . . music school? Are you going to be a music teacher?

10 **REBECCA** Maybe . . . or a performer or a songwriter, or all three.

11 **AUNT MOLLY** Your mother always wanted to be a singer.

12 **PRINCIPAL** Kevin Patrick Casey.

13 *Kevin receives his diploma. After, he and Laura talk to her parents. Rebecca, Dad, and Aunt Molly wait*
14 *for Kevin.*

15 **DAD**   Kevin! Over here.

16 **KEVIN**   (*Kevin is talking to several people.*) Oh, that's my dad. I gotta go . . . I'll see you later.

17 **REBECCA** Congratulations!

18 *He joins his family as everyone congratulates him. Rebecca takes the family photo. Everyone is proud*
19 *of Kevin.*

20 **REBECCA** All right, stand over there. I want to get a picture. You too, Aunt Molly.
21   All right, look this way. Say cheese!

22 **KEVIN**   Cheese! (*She takes the picture.*)

23 **DAD**   Kevin, I'm proud to see that diploma in your hand.

24 **MOLLY**   We all are. Congratulations, Kevin.

25 **KEVIN**   Thanks.

26 **REBECCA** Dad, stand next to Kevin. I want to get a picture of just the two of you.

27 *Dad joins Kevin and Aunt Molly stands beside Rebecca as she takes a picture.*

28 **MOLLY**   And I'm proud of you, too, Becky.

29 **REBECCA** Me? Why?

30 **MOLLY**   Don't be so modest. When your mother died, you . . . you stepped right in and
31   you became the mother. You took good care of Kevin and your Dad.

32 **REBECCA** Well . . . there was no one else.

PART 2

33 *REBECCA'S ROOM—NIGHT*

34 *Rebecca comes through the door from work. She has a letter from the Boston School of Music. She takes it*
35 *to her room. She sits down on the bed, takes a deep breath, and opens the letter. She reads it quietly. It is a*
36 *rejection letter.*

37 **REBECCA** *(reading the letter)* We are sorry to inform you . . . Oh, no. I can't believe it . . . God
38 . . . another rejection letter.

39 *Rebecca feels bad. She lies back on the bed and wonders what she will do next.*

40 **REBECCA** Three rejections. I can't believe it.

41 *FACTORY—MORNING*

42 *Rebecca and Sandy work for a company that manufactures computers. They are walking and talking.*

43 **SANDY** Three rejections. I can't believe it. What are you going to do?

44 **REBECCA** I'm waiting to hear from one more school. They put me on their waiting list.
45 Keep your fingers crossed. *(She crosses her fingers.)*

46 **SANDY** Only one? Well, I hope they take you.

47 **REBECCA** I'm supposed to hear this week.

48 **SANDY** Which college—the New England Conservatory?

49 **REBECCA** No, they turned me down. It's the San Francisco College of Music.

50 **SANDY** San Francisco?

51 **REBECCA** That's right. San Francisco, California.

52 **SANDY** Rebecca!

53 *FACTORY, LUNCHROOM*

54 **SANDY** But, Rebecca, this school is on the other side of the country.

55 **REBECCA** I know that, but if San Francisco accepts me and gives me some financial aid,
56 that's where I'm going.

57 **SANDY** But you don't know a soul out there.

58 **REBECCA** Yes, I do. My godmother lives out there.

59 *She shows Sandy a picture of her godmother standing in front of a lovely Victorian house.*

60 **SANDY** What is she, rich or something? She has such a big house.

61 **REBECCA** No, she's not rich, but she does have room for me if I get accepted.

62 **SANDY** You're really serious about this, aren't you?

63 **REBECCA** Dead serious.

64 *REBECCA'S BEDROOM—NIGHT*

65 *We see a brochure from the San Francisco College of Music and a map of the U.S. Rebecca is figuring out a*
66 *route from Boston to San Francisco. Kevin knocks on Rebecca's door.*

67 **REBECCA** Come in.

68 **KEVIN** When do we eat?

69 REBECCA   In five minutes. Dinner's in the oven.

70 KEVIN   Dad's not eating. He went to bed.

71 REBECCA   What's wrong? Is he sick?

72 KEVIN   No. He just said he was tired.

73 *Kevin notices what Rebecca is doing. He stops and asks his sister about her plans.*

74 KEVIN   So, did you hear anything about your applications . . . you know, to music school?

75 REBECCA   I got three rejection letters.

76 KEVIN   That's too bad. So, what're you going to do?

77 REBECCA   I still have one last hope . . . a school in San Francisco.

78 *Rebecca hands him the brochure.*

79 KEVIN   (shocked) San Francisco . . .

80 *Rebecca smiles at him to get him into a good mood. She crosses her fingers. He smiles too and crosses his*
81 *fingers.*

PART 3

82 CASEY APARTMENT, KITCHEN—EARLY MORNING

83 *Rebecca is getting ready to go to work. Rebecca's father is dressed in pajamas. He is sitting and reading*
84 *the newspaper.*

85 DAD   (sounding as if he's in pain) Ow-oo.

86 REBECCA   What, Dad? Are you OK?

87 DAD   (making a joke) No! . . . The Red Sox lost another game.

88 REBECCA   Dad, you make me crazy. Is my purse out there?

89 DAD   (He sees it on the table.) Yeah. It's here.

90 *Rebecca comes rushing in and grabs her purse. Dad picks up the San Francisco College brochure.*

91 DAD   (holding the brochure) What's this?

92 *Rebecca takes back the brochure and puts it into her purse.*

93 REBECCA   A college brochure. See you tonight.

94 *Rebecca is leaving the kitchen when Dad yells to her.*

95 DAD   Becky, pick up the mail, OK?

96 REBECCA   Pick up the mail? It's too early.

97 DAD   Yesterday's mail.

98 REBECCA   But, Dad, you always get the mail . . .

99 DAD   Well, I didn't yesterday. My leg was bothering me.

100 *She leaves and he takes out his pills from his bathrobe pocket.*

101 FRONT OF THE CASEY APARTMENT BUILDING

102 *Mrs. Peterson is returning home after taking her dog, Trixy, for a walk. Rebecca picks up the mail.*

103 **MRS. PETERSON** Oh, Trixy, that was a great walk. Here we are. Home again! Good morning,
104   Rebecca. How are you?

105 **REBECCA** Good morning, Mrs. Peterson. Hi, Trixy.

106 **MRS. PETERSON** Is the mail here already?

107 **REBECCA** No. This is from yesterday.

108 **MRS. PETERSON** Oh. Excuse us.

109 *She sees her name on an envelope. It's from the San Francisco College of Music. She rips it open and*
110 *quickly reads it.*

111 **REBECCA** *(talking to herself)* San Francisco! We are pleased to inform you that you have been
112   accepted at the San Francisco . . . Oh, my God! I'm going . . .

113 **MRS. PETERSON** Good news?

114 **REBECCA** *(excited)* I . . . I . . . very good news.

115 FACTORY—MORNING

116 *Rebecca punches in at the time clock and rushes off. Workers look at each other. They wonder what's going*
117 *on.*

118 **REBECCA** Hi . . . !

119 **WORKER #1** What's up with Rebecca?

120 **JUDY** I don't know.

121 **WORKER #2** Well, she certainly seems happy.

122 **REBECCA** Good morning, Grace. *(Rebecca rushes up to Sandy.)*

123 **REBECCA** Sandy, I got the letter! I'm in!

124 **SANDY** What letter? You mean, the San Francisco school?

125 **REBECCA** Look! *(She hands her the letter. Sandy reads it out loud.)*

126 **SANDY** *(reading the letter)* Dear Ms. Casey: Congratulations! . . . Oh my gosh, they
127   accepted you! The San Francisco College of Music! . . . Oh, Rebecca . . . I'm so
128   happy for you!

129 **REBECCA** Can you believe it?

130 *The two women hug and laugh.*

131 FACTORY LUNCH ROOM—NOON

132 *Workers are talking and eating together. Judy is talking to another worker. That worker glances over at the*
133 *table where Rebecca is sitting and talking with Sandy.*

134 **JUDY** Guess what? Rebecca's going to college.

135 **WORKER #1** College! . . . Good for her.

136 **JUDY** And she's quitting her job, too, and moving to San Francisco.

137 **WORKER #1** She's quitting?

138 **JUDY** Would you give up your job in this economy? No way.

139 **WORKER #1** Well, it's Rebecca's dream. It's good to have dreams. *(Judy shakes her head.)*

140 *BUS STOP*

141 *Rebecca and Sandy get on the bus and then sit together on the bus.*

142 **REBECCA**   I've got an idea! Why don't you come to San Francisco with me!

143 **SANDY**   San Francisco? . . . I don't think so.

144 **REBECCA**   Why not?

145 **SANDY**   Well, first of all, I don't have any money.

146 **REBECCA**   I'll lend you some.

147 **SANDY**   Don't be silly. You're not Rockefeller.

148 **REBECCA**   Come on. What's keeping you in Boston? Nothing!

149 **SANDY**   Ain't that the truth . . . but it is home . . . I mean, my mother lives here . . .

150 **REBECCA**   You and your mom don't even talk.

151 **SANDY**   Well . . . there's Jack . . .

152 **REBECCA**   Right . . . you and Jack—you know what I think about that!

153
154 **SANDY**   But it's still home. Sorry, Rebecca, Boston's my town. Nice of you to ask, but no thanks.

155 **REBECCA**   Well, it was an idea.

156 **SANDY**   San Francisco. Wait till Matt and your dad hear about this!

157 *Rebecca nods her head.*

158 CASEY APARTMENT, KITCHEN—NIGHT

159 *Dad is sitting in the kitchen sipping water while taking some pills. He hears the door open and quickly puts*
160 *the bottle of pills in his pocket. He sits down at the table pretending to read. Rebecca enters. She's carrying*
161 *the letter.*

162 **REBECCA**   Dad?

163 **DAD**   Yeah?

164 **REBECCA**   We have to talk.

. . . . EPISODE **5** . . . .

Breaking the News

PART 1

1 CASEY APARTMENT, KITCHEN—NIGHT

2 *Dad is sitting in the kitchen sipping water while taking some pills. He hears the door open and quickly puts*
3 *the bottle of pills in his pocket. Rebecca enters. She's carrying the letter.*

4 **REBECCA**   Dad?

5 **DAD**   Yeah?

6 **REBECCA**   We have to talk.

7 **DAD**   Uh-huh.

8 *Rebecca sits down across the table from her dad. She smiles, and then he smiles, a little bit afraid.*

9 **REBECCA**   I have some good news.

10 **DAD**   Oh?

11 **REBECCA**   This music school accepted me and they're offering financial aid and a partial
12   scholarship. I . . . uh . . . they want me to be a student there.

13 *He takes the letter from her.*

14 **DAD**   When did you get this letter?

15 **REBECCA**   This morning.

16 *He reads quickly and is shocked.*

17 **DAD**   This college is in San Francisco!

18 **REBECCA**   Yeah, I know.

19 **DAD**   My God, that's the other side of the earth!

20 **REBECCA**   Come on, Dad. It's only six hours by plane.

21 **DAD**   It's too far away. We'll never see you. Why don't you go to school around here?

22 **REBECCA**   All the music schools in Boston turned me down.

23 **DAD**   What about a nice community college . . . a good teacher's college . . .

24 **REBECCA**   I want to study music. This is the only music school that accepted me.

25 **DAD**   What about Kevin? What about us?

26 **REBECCA**   Kevin's almost eighteen; he can take care of himself. And with a little help from
27   him, you'll be fine, too. This is my big chance.

28 *Kevin hears something going on and comes over to the kitchen entrance. He listens to his sister and father*
29 *talk.*

30 **DAD**   So, what do you want from me?

31 **REBECCA**   I . . . um . . . nothing. Just your approval.

32 **DAD**   You want my approval? No way.

33 **REBECCA**   What?

34 **DAD**   *(spelling)* N-O. No way.

35 **REBECCA**   That's it? End of conversation?

36 **DAD**   What do you want me to say . . . that I'm thrilled? I gave you my opinion, but
37   you don't care.

38 **REBECCA**   But, Dad. This is something I really want to do.

39 **DAD**   There's a lot I want to do, too. But you don't always get what you want in this
40   world.

41 **REBECCA**   But, I'm not going forever. I'll call. I'll visit.

42 **DAD**   Visit? Who's gonna pay for that?

43 **REBECCA**   I will.

44	DAD	And where are you going to live out there? Rebecca, do you know how expensive
45		it is to live on your own?
46	REBECCA	Yes, I do. I have a place to stay.
47	DAD	(*He looks afraid.*) I don't understand . . .
48	REBECCA	Rent-free.
49	DAD	Where?
50	REBECCA	At Nancy Shaw's. (*Dad looks at her for a moment and starts to leave.*)
51	DAD	That woman! Where's my cane?
52	REBECCA	I know you don't like Nancy, but she is my godmother.

53 *He grabs his cane and stands up.*

54	DAD	Does your brother know about this?
55	REBECCA	Not yet.
56	DAD	I'm going to bed.

57 *He walks out of the kitchen. Rebecca is left alone. She looks tired and upset. Kevin enters. She realizes that*
58 *he has heard everything.*

59	KEVIN	That school in San Francisco accepted you?
60	REBECCA	Yeah. They gave me financial aid, too . . .
61	KEVIN	So what are you gonna do?
62	REBECCA	Dad really wants me to stay, but I'm going.
63	KEVIN	When do you have to leave?
64	REBECCA	In a few weeks. (*Kevin is surprised.*) Kev, the truth. Is it all right with you if I go?
65	KEVIN	(*after a pause*) Go for it! (*She hugs him.*)
66	REBECCA	Thanks . . . You're a pal.
67	KEVIN	Don't worry about Dad. He'll get used to it.
68	REBECCA	You think so?
69	KEVIN	I'm sure of it . . . Besides, then I can have your room.
70	REBECCA	My room! You little . . . my room! I'm not even out of here yet and you want my
71		room?

72 *They laugh together.*

73 *DAD'S BEDROOM*

74 *He enters his room and we can hear Kevin and Rebecca from the other room. He just closes the door.*

PART 2

75 *FACTORY—MORNING*

76 *The factory is a busy place. Sandy pulls Rebecca away from work.*

| 77 | SANDY | It's ten o'clock. Come on. It's break time. |
| 78 | REBECCA | You want to get a soda? |

79	**SANDY**	No. I need a cigarette.
80	**REBECCA**	No, you don't.
81	**SANDY**	Yes, I do.
82	**REBECCA**	Sandy, when are you going to quit smoking?
83	**SANDY**	Tomorrow. (*Rebecca shakes her head.*)

84 *Workers are standing outside taking their break. Rebecca and Sandy are sitting and talking.*

85	**SANDY**	So? What did they say?
86	**REBECCA**	I haven't told Matt. Kevin thinks it's great. My dad is definitely not happy!
87	**SANDY**	He's mad, huh?
88	**REBECCA**	Yeah . . . Well, today's the day. It's time to let the boss know I'm leaving.
89	**SANDY**	You're going to quit . . . just like that?
90	**REBECCA**	Well, I have to give them a two-week notice, right? Then . . . I'm out of here.
91	**SANDY**	Oh, I can't believe it.
92 93	**REBECCA**	Well, it's true . . . Hey, I need some new clothes . . . you want to go shopping after work?
94	**SANDY**	OK.

95 *SHOPPING MALL—AFTERNOON*

96 *Rebecca and Sandy walk through the mall. They go into a clothing store. Rebecca is looking through a rack*
97 *of dresses. The rack is clearly marked "Sale."*

98	**SANDY**	What are we looking for?
99 100	**REBECCA**	I've got plenty of jeans and casual stuff for class. What I really need is something dressy for California. I've got zilch. (*Sandy pulls out a beautiful silk dress.*)
101	**SANDY**	How about this?
102	**REBECCA**	Too formal. (*Rebecca pulls a dress from the rack.*) This is pretty. Where's the price tag?

103 *Rebecca finds the tag.*

104	**REBECCA**	Two hundred dollars! And it's on sale?
105	**SANDY**	Who can afford this stuff? (*Rebecca finds another dress and looks for the tag.*)
106	**REBECCA**	This is 30 percent off—only sixty dollars.
107	**SANDY**	I like it. Do they have your size?
108	**REBECCA**	Mmm . . . Size six, perfect. I'm going to try it on.

109 *Sandy is outside dressing area. She talks to Rebecca, who is changing clothes inside.*

110	**SANDY**	Listen, I have to tell you a big secret. My mom doesn't even know.
111	**REBECCA**	What?
112	**SANDY**	I'm moving in with Jack.
113 114	**REBECCA**	You're what? (*She sticks her head out of the dressing room.*) The two of you are always fighting!
115	**SANDY**	Well . . . things change.

116 **REBECCA** Yeah, but people don't.

117 **SANDY** Look, I'm going to do it. Period. I know you don't think it's a good idea, so let's
118 just change the subject.

119 *Rebecca comes out of the dressing room. She is wearing a yellow dress.*

120 **REBECCA** Sandy, I just want you to be happy, that's all. This thing with you and Jack is just . . .

121 **SANDY** Look . . . I think I can make it work.

122 *Rebecca stands in front of the mirror. She looks at herself in the new dress.*

123 **SANDY** It looks great.

124 **REBECCA** I don't know. Maybe it's too . . .

125 **SANDY** It's perfect.

126 **REBECCA** All right.

127 *Rebecca and Sandy are carrying coffee and shopping bags. They walk to a table and sit down.*

128 **SANDY** When do you have to leave?

129 **REBECCA** In a few weeks.

130 **SANDY** Do you have your plane ticket?

131 **REBECCA** No, of course not.

132 **SANDY** You'd better hurry up. It's cheaper if you buy your ticket a few weeks in advance.

133 **REBECCA** I'm not flying; I'm driving to San Francisco.

134 **SANDY** Drive? All by yourself? Are you crazy?

135 **REBECCA** No, practical. I'll need a car in San Francisco, right? Anyway, I want to see the
136 Southwest. So, why not buy a car here and drive it out there?

137 **SANDY** You are nuts! So, what kind of car are you gonna get?

138 **REBECCA** The best car I can get for fifteen hundred dollars.

PART 3

139 *USED CAR LOT—MORNING*

140 *Kevin and Rebecca are looking at cars at a used car lot. They walk up to cars, look inside, and read the*
141 *stickers on each car. A salesman approaches them. He has a Boston accent.*

142 **SALESMAN** Hello. Can I help you folks?

143 **REBECCA** We're just looking, thanks.

144 **SALESMAN** Are you looking for anything special?

145 **KEVIN** She's looking for a car to drive across country.

146 **SALESMAN** Gotcha! So you want something you can count on . . .

147 **REBECCA** Yeah. (*Rebecca nods as she continues to look at a car.*)

148 **SALESMAN** I have something for you right over here . . . It's in A-1 condition. New tires,
149 excellent engine . . . It's a Florida car.

150 *The three of them walk over. The salesman taps the hood. Rebecca looks. It's a relatively new model. She*
151 *looks at the sticker price and is quite shocked.*

152 **REBECCA**   Oh, no! That's much too expensive . . . (*She looks at Kevin.*)

153 **SALESMAN**   Well, for you, I can come down a little in the price. How much do you want to
154   spend?

155 *Rebecca doesn't want to name her limit, but then she says it.*

156 **REBECCA**   Fifteen hundred, max.

157 **SALESMAN**   Fifteen hundred, max!!!!! I don't think so . . . I haven't really got anything for
158   you . . . But I've got a friend who sells cars about four blocks from here . . .

159 *CASEY APARTMENT—EVENING*

160 *Dad is sitting in the apartment doing a crossword puzzle. Rebecca and Kevin enter. Dad looks up briefly and*
161 *returns to the puzzle.*

162 **KEVIN**   I need something to eat. Do you want anything?

163 **REBECCA**   No, thanks.

164 *Kevin goes into the kitchen. Rebecca goes into the living room to talk with her father.*

165 **REBECCA**   Hi.

166 **DAD**   Hi.

167 *Rebecca comes and sits next to her father.*

168 **REBECCA**   Kevin and I went looking at used cars . . . for my trip. They're all so expensive.

169 **DAD**   Unh-huh.

170 **REBECCA**   This is silly. Would you please talk to me? (*He puts down his paper.*)

171 **DAD**   OK.

172 **REBECCA**   Everyone has to leave home . . . sometime.

173 *Her father does not respond. Rebecca tries harder.*

174 **REBECCA**   Dad, I'm leaving pretty soon.

175 **DAD**   I know.

176 **REBECCA**   I don't want to leave with you angry at me.

177 **DAD**   I'm not angry.

178 **REBECCA**   Try to be happy for me.

179 **DAD**   I just don't see why you have to go so far away.

180 **REBECCA**   Dad, it's something I really want to do . . .

181 **DAD**   I know, I know. But I don't have to like it, do I?

182 *Dad continues reading his paper. Rebecca looks sad. She is tired of trying.*

EPISODE

6

· ·

Saying Goodbye

PART 1

1 COMMUNITY CENTER—DAY

2 *A young girl, late for her guitar lesson, heads toward the classroom where Rebecca is waiting for her.*

3 **MELISSA** Hi, Miss Casey. I'm sorry I'm late for my lesson.

4 **REBECCA** Hi, Melissa, how are you doing?

5 **MELISSA** Fine.

6 **REBECCA** Good. (*Melissa sits down and takes her guitar out of its case.*) Listen, before we begin, I
7 have to tell you something.

8 **MELISSA** What?

9 **REBECCA** I'm going back to school.

10 **MELISSA** You are? Why?

11 **REBECCA** To study music.

12 **MELISSA** But you're the best music teacher, and you know lots of music.

13 **REBECCA** Thanks, but I want to be better . . . But I'm sad because the school is far away
14 and I won't be . . .

15 **MELISSA** Where is it?

16 **REBECCA** San Francisco.

17 **MELISSA** Where's that?

18 *Rebecca goes to the map of the U.S. and shows Melissa where it is.*

19 **REBECCA** We're here . . . and San Francisco's all the way over here, in California.

20 **MELISSA** I won't be able to see you?

21 **REBECCA** Yes, I'm leaving, but, let's see, we have one more lesson. I'll try to find you a good
22 teacher, OK?

23 **MELISSA** (*sadly nodding*) OK.

24 **REBECCA** What do you want to play first?

25 **MELISSA** Can we play the blues?

26 **REBECCA** Sure. You know 'Travelin' Blues,' right?

27 **MELISSA** Yeah.

28 **REBECCA** Let's play that.

29 **MELISSA** OK.

30 **REBECCA** 'A' Major.

31 *The girl starts to play some simple music and then Rebecca starts to play on her guitar. The two smile at*
32 *each other.*

PART 2

33 *USED CAR LOT—DAY*

34 *Dad and his friend, Frank Wells, are walking around the used car lot looking at cars. The cars have prices*
35 *on them.*

36 **DAD**   What do you think, Frank . . . am I nuts?

37 **FRANK**   No, you're not crazy. Rebecca's twenty-eight. I mean, it's about time she got a car.

38 *The two men walk and look at another car.*

39 **FRANK**   Hey, what do you think of this one here?

40 **DAD**   No way! Look at the price!

41 **FRANK**   She needs a small car—something she can drive around Boston.

42 **DAD**   Frank . . . she's driving all the way to San Francisco.

43 **FRANK**   San Francisco?

44 **DAD**   Yeah, alone.

45 **FRANK**   She's gonna drive three thousand miles . . . by herself? . . . Is that safe?

46 **DAD**   I think she should fly if she insists on going, but she said she'd rather put the
47   money in a car that she can use when she's out there.

48 **FRANK**   I'd never drive that far by myself. Ya know that daughter of yours is pretty
49   independent. Hey, now here's a car to drive across country in.

50 *Franks pauses to look at a car.*

51 **DAD**   She got into a good school, Frank. The San Francisco College of Music.

52 *Mr. Casey follows him to another car.*

53 **FRANK**   Music school? That'll never pay off. You can't make any money in music.

54 **DAD**   You're telling me! I thought she should go to a local college.

55 **FRANK**   Well, that makes more sense to me. So why does she have to go all the way to
56   San Francisco?

57 **DAD**   Well, the school out there accepted her . . . and they offered her financial help.

58 **FRANK**   Well that's good, right?

59 **DAD**   I guess so.

60 *Frank turns and looks Dad in the eye.*

61 **FRANK**   Hey, if you're so worried about this, why don't you talk her out of it?

62 **DAD**   I can't change her mind. She's all fired up about the idea. Says it's her dream.

63 **FRANK**   Yeah, but dreams don't pay bills.

64 **DAD**   Yeah, well there's nothing I can do . . . If this is what she wants, maybe I can help
65   her with a car.

66 **FRANK**   Well, if she's gonna be drivin', ya know, all the way across country, she's gotta
67   have a decent car.

68 **FRANK**   Hey . . . hey, here's one of those—what-do-you-call-it—Oldsmobile Deltas?

69 *Dad walks over and looks in.*

70	DAD	Yeah, Oldsmobile Delta. *(looking it over)*
71	FRANK	Hey, looks in tip-top shape, look.
72 DAD		Oh, you don't know about used cars, Frank. *(looking at the mileage)* Whew! 80,000
73		miles.
74 FRANK		Oh, that's a lot of miles! You know we have to take a close look at the engine,
75		the tires, the doors, everything . . .
76	DAD	*(looking at the sticker price)* It's a lot of money, Frank. I don't wanna get ripped off.
77	FRANK	You have to watch these used car salesmen.
78	DAD	I don't know . . . Do I wanna do this?
79	FRANK	She'll love ya for it.
80	DAD	You think so?
81	FRANK	Yeah . . . there, c'mon, let's take a look.

82 *Frank lifts the hood and they look in. The hood is heavy. It almost falls on Frank's hand.*

83	FRANK	Whew, watch that one . . . Hey, looks clean, no oil leaks.
84 DAD		That's a lotta mileage, Frank . . . Let's have that mechanic of yours, what's
85		his name . . .
86	FRANK	Sammy?
87	DAD	Yeah.
88 FRANK		Yeah. We'll tell the salesman we want our mechanic to take a look at it before we
89		pay anything.
90	DAD	And we take it for a test drive, too.
91	FRANK	You got it. *(The two men start walking back to the sales office.)*
92	DAD	*(taking a deep breath)* OK. Let's make a deal.

PART 3

93 *BASEBALL FIELD—AFTERNOON*

94 *Sandy and Kevin are watching Rebecca and her friends play baseball. Kevin's eating potato chips.*

95	SANDY	What's the score?
96	KEVIN	Three to nothing.
97	SANDY	Three to nothing?

98 *A woman on the opposing team approaches home plate. Rebecca and others cheer on the pitcher.*

99	REBECCA	All right, Mary!
100 PLAYER		C'mon, Mary. You can do it, Mary. Put it right by her now, Mary. C'mon, she's no
101		batter, let's go Mary!

102 *Sandy and Kevin stand to cheer for Rebecca.*

| 103 | SANDY | That a girl, Becky! |
| 104 | KEVIN | Come on, Becky, beat the bums! |

105 *Sandy reaches over and takes some potato chips.*

106	SANDY	So how do you feel about Rebecca leaving home?
107	KEVIN	Uh, I don't know. I'm OK, I guess.
108	SANDY	You're going to miss her, aren't you?
109 KEVIN 110		Yeah, but at least I get to move into her room. Hey, don't take all my potato chips!
111	SANDY	Don't be so stingy!

112 *Rebecca yells, trying to get the team going.*

| 113 | REBECCA | Come on, girl—put it in there, one more out! Let's go, Mary! |

114 *The ball is hit directly at Rebecca. She catches it and makes a play to first. The umpire calls the runner safe.*
115 *She and her teammates argue that the umpire's decision was wrong.*

116	UMPIRE	Safe!
117	REBECCA	She is not!
118	UMPIRE	Is too.
119	REBECCA	Is not.
120	UMPIRE	Safe. End of discussion. (*The team groans.*)
121	REBECCA	Oh, this is ridiculous, she was . . . she was out, there was no . . . (*sigh*)

122 *Rebecca walks off very unhappy. The scoreboard reads: 22 to 2. The team walks off the field after the*
123 *game. Kevin and Sandy walk away with Rebecca. She is disappointed at the score.*

124	KEVIN	Twenty-two to two, what happened to you? (*Rebecca gives him an unhappy look.*)
125	REBECCA	Hey, how 'bout a little sympathy? I lost my last softball game.
126	SANDY	Poor you! You can't do it all by yourself. If it wasn't for that umpire . . .
127	KEVIN	Yeah, I think he was working for the other team.
128	REBECCA	What the heck, it's only a game, right?
129	KEVIN	I think I'm heading home. I'll see you later.
130	REBECCA	All right, thanks for coming.
131	KEVIN	Oh, it was fun . . . seeing you get beat!
132	REBECCA	(*taking a swing at him with her glove*) You're supposed to be cheering me on . . .
133	KEVIN	Tomorrow night we'll go car hunting again?
134	REBECCA	Absolutely . . . Bye.
135	KEVIN	Bye, Sandy.
136	SANDY	Bye! Thanks for the potato chips!
137	REBECCA	Hey, the team's going to the Sports Bar, do you wanna come?
138	SANDY	I can't. Jack and I are going to the movies.
139	REBECCA	I still don't know what you see in that guy.
140	SANDY	You're not me, OK?

141 *It is clear that Sandy is sensitive about the subject of Jack.*

| 142 | SANDY | Now, when are you leaving for San Francisco? |

143 **REBECCA**   A week from Saturday. I drive out real early.

144 **SANDY**   Let's hope you have a car by then . . .

145 **REBECCA**   I will!

146 *SPORTS BAR—EVENING*

147 *At a big table, Rebecca's team is having a good old time. Rebecca is happy, but sad about moving to San*
148 *Francisco and leaving her friends. Rebecca's friend brings a present out from under the table. She wants to*
149 *put it in front of Rebecca, but the table is crowded.*

150 **PITCHER**   Oh, make room, move that glove.

151 *PLAYER #2 picks up Rebecca's glove and glass, and the popcorn. PLAYER #1 places the present in front of*
152 *Rebecca.*

153 **REBECCA**   Oh my gosh! You guys, you didn't have to do this, this is too much!

154 **PLAYER**   Open the card first.

155 **REBECCA**   *(smiling as she shakes the box curiously)* OK.

156 *The friends laugh. Rebecca reads the card aloud.*

157 **REBECCA**   'You're in our hearts, as you well know . . .
158   We'll think of you, wherever you go.
159   You'll be a hit in San Francis-co!'
160   *(smiling at everyone)* Thanks.

161 **PLAYER**   OK, hurry up, hurry up!

162 **REBECCA**   *(opening the box)* What did you guys get me?

163 *Everyone cheers as Rebecca rips open her present. She pulls out a Red Sox baseball jacket.*

164 **REBECCA**   *(surprised)* A Red Sox jacket! This is great!

165 *The players admire the jacket as she puts it on.*

166 **REBECCA**   What a great present. Thanks, you guys! Ah, what to say . . . Well, we didn't win
167   many games, but we had more fun than any other team in the league . . . and I'm
168   never gonna forget the Silver Stars. I'm gonna miss you guys.

169 *Rebecca looks around, feeling her friends' affection. The team pats her on the back and hugs her.*

170 **REBECCA**   Don't replace me too soon, OK?

171 *The whole group laughs.*

172 *OUTSIDE THE SPORTS BAR*

173 *Matt is sitting on the hood of his car, which is parked in front of the Sports Bar. Rebecca comes out, wearing*
174 *her Red Sox jacket. She is talking with a few teammates. She notices Matt for the first time.*

175 **REBECCA**   Hey, Matt! What are you doing here?

176 **MATT**   I got out of work late. I called your house. And Kevin told me you'd be here.
177   Nice jacket.

178 **REBECCA**   Thanks, it's a present from the team.

179 **MATT**   They're gonna miss you. You're their star player.

180 **REBECCA**   I wasn't today. We lost, twenty-two to two.

181	MATT	Ouch. *(pause)* I think we need to have a talk.
182	REBECCA	Look, if it's about my decision to go to San Francisco, I'm not going to change my
183		mind.
184	MATT	I realize that.
185	REBECCA	But I'll be back to visit . . . and you can come and see me.

186 *Matt shakes his head.*

187	MATT	No, let's not kid ourselves. Four years of college in California will pretty much
188		end our relationship.
189	REBECCA	Lots of people have long-distance relationships.
190	MATT	Not me. I'm not a long-distance kind of guy. All our friends are getting married.
191		They're having kids. I thought we were next.

192 *Rebecca is silent. She looks away.*

193	MATT	See, Becky, you and I . . . we have different dreams . . . I think it's better to call it
194		quits.
195	REBECCA	*(sadly)* Is it?
196	MATT	I think so.
197	REBECCA	Look, I'm sorry you feel this way, but I'm never going to be happy if I don't try
198		this. I'm sorry.

199 *She walks away.*

EPISODE
7

Leaving Home

PART 1

1 CASEY APARTMENT—MORNING

2 *Dad is standing next to the car he purchased with Frank Wells. Dad looks up and waves, sending a signal*
3 *that he's ready. Kevin is standing at the window. Kevin leaves the window. He walks to Rebecca's door and*
4 *knocks.*

5 KEVIN Rebecca, Dad wants to see you.

6 REBECCA I'm on the phone.

7 *Kevin leaves the door with a big smile on his face. The door opens and Rebecca is talking on a*
8 *cordless phone.*

9 REBECCA *(on the phone)* I'll write to you from California . . . I'll see you when I come home.
10 Goodbye, Aunt Molly. Take care.

11 *Rebecca hangs up the phone and then she wonders what her father wants. She walks through the house*
12 *looking for her father. She goes into the kitchen, back to her father's room, checking every place in the small*
13 *apartment.*

14 REBECCA Dad? . . . Kevin, where are you?

15 **KEVIN**   Rebecca!

16 **REBECCA** What?

17 **KEVIN**   I'm in the kitchen.

18 *Rebecca goes to the kitchen door.*

19 **REBECCA** What's going on?

20 **KEVIN**   Dad's downstairs. He wants to show you something.

21 **REBECCA** Show me? Show me what?

22 **KEVIN**   You'll see. Come on.

23 *Kevin leads Rebecca to the porch stairs.*

24 **REBECCA** Kevin, I'm busy packing. What's this all about?

25 **KEVIN**   Ask Dad.

26 *OUTSIDE THE CASEY APARTMENT*

27 *Rebecca sees her father standing next to a car. Dad holds up the keys.*

28 **REBECCA** What's this?

29 **DAD**   *(holding up the keys)* It's your new car.

30 **REBECCA** *(She walks up to the car.)* Dad! You're joking!

31 *Rebecca can't believe it is her car. Rebecca looks at her dad.*

32 **REBECCA** I . . . I can't believe it! This is for me?

33 **DAD**   *(interrupting)* You need a car, don't you? . . . And you deserve it. It's a little present
34   from Kevin and me.

35 *She hugs her father and now she realizes that he has finally given his blessing to her trip.*

36 **DAD**   Ugh! Not so tight!

37 *When she releases him, he gives her some documents.*

38 **DAD**   And here's the title to the car *(hands her the title)*, and I paid for the car insurance.

39 **REBECCA** I'm . . . just speechless.

40 **DAD**   You . . . speechless? Kevin, when's the last time your sister was speechless?

41 **KEVIN**   Not in a long time. So are we goin' for a ride?

42 *She climbs in and sits in her car. A big smile breaks across her face.*

43 **DAD**   What do ya think?

44 **REBECCA** It's perfect. My first car . . . I can't believe it!

45 **KEVIN**   So?

46 **REBECCA** Get in!

47 *BOSTON STREET*

48 *The three Caseys are enjoying Rebecca's new used car.*

49 **REBECCA** This car's great, Dad, but I bet you spent a fortune on it!

50 **DAD**   Not really. I got a good deal.

51	**KEVIN**	Try the horn. (*Rebecca blows the horn.*)
52	**DAD**	It's got a good radio and tape deck . . . everything a musician needs on a long
53		trip . . . (*looking at the Boston skyline*) Look at that view.
54	**REBECCA**	I'm gonna miss this place.
55	**DAD**	Sure y'are. Boston's been your home for twenty-eight years.
56	**REBECCA**	When I think about leaving, I get butterflies in my stomach.
57	**DAD**	You'll be fine.
58	**KEVIN**	Yeah, you'll be OK.
59	**REBECCA**	I hope so.

PART 2

60 *REBECCA'S ROOM—AFTERNOON*

61 *Rebecca is packing her clothes. Her door is open and Kevin appears.*

62	**KEVIN**	You're talking to yourself.
63	**REBECCA**	It's an old habit.
64	**KEVIN**	Boy, you have a lot of bags.
65	**REBECCA**	Maybe I shouldn't take all this stuff. Well, but what if I need it? (*She is packing a*
66		*suitcase.*)
67	**KEVIN**	I hope we can fit all these suitcases into the car.
68	**REBECCA**	We have to! . . . Oh, I have some things to show you. Here's a list of what needs
69		to be done on a regular basis . . . put out the garbage, recycle the glass and the
70		cans, the newspapers and the cardboard . . . don't put anything . . .
71	**KEVIN**	Dad's on my case about all of that.
72	**REBECCA**	You need to help him keep the place clean, buy the groceries . . .
73	**KEVIN**	I'm starting to realize how nice it is to have a big sister around. (*Rebecca smiles at*
74		*Kevin.*) It's gonna be kind of strange without you.

75 *They look at each other. She steps over and hugs him. He returns the hug.*

76 *CASEY APARTMENT—NIGHT*

77 *Dad is wrapping something at the kitchen table. He starts coughing.*

78 *Rebecca's in her bedroom. She finally gives herself a break, picks up her guitar, and starts a little song.*
79 *There's a knock on the door. It's her father. She stops playing.*

| 80 | **REBECCA** | Hi. |

81 *The door opens. We can see him shift a small, wrapped present from in front of him to behind his back.*
82 *Rebecca doesn't notice.*

83	**DAD**	Are you all packed?
84	**REBECCA**	Almost.
85	**DAD**	I want you to have this. (*He hands her a package.*)
86	**REBECCA**	Dad . . . another present? (*She starts to open it.*) What is it? (*She pulls out a simple gold*
87		*necklace.*) Mom's necklace. Do you really want me to have this?

88 *Dad nods. Rebecca stands and walks to the mirror over her dresser. She puts it on.*

89 REBECCA (*looking in the mirror*) It's beautiful. Thanks, Dad.

90 DAD I'm sorry your mother isn't here to say all the right things . . . so I'll try, myself.

91 REBECCA (*interrupting*) It's OK, Dad, you don't have to . . .

92 DAD This is your home . . . If you ever need help . . . or change your mind . . . or
93 anything . . . remember, we're here.

94 REBECCA Thanks, Dad. Thanks for everything . . . I love you . . . (*She hugs him.*)

95 DAD (*patting her on the back*) I'll miss ya, God knows.

96 *They pull apart.*

97 DAD Well, you'd better get some sleep. You've got a big day tomorrow.

98 REBECCA 'Night, Dad.

99 DAD 'Night.

100 *He walks off into the darkness turning off the hall light. Rebecca looks at her mother's picture in the mirror.*

PART 3

101 OUTSIDE THE CASEY APARTMENT—MORNING

102 *Kevin is loading up the car with suitcases. Several suitcases sit on the sidewalk.*

103 DAD For crying out loud. Your sister won't be able to see!

104 KEVIN (*He moves some of the bags in the back seat.*) All right already! Are there any
105 more bags?

106 DAD (*pointing to the suitcases near the car*) No, this is it.

107 KEVIN I'll put these in the trunk.

108 DAD OK.

109 *Sandy comes hurrying up the street, carrying a present.*

110 SANDY Hey, guys, where is she?

111 KEVIN Don't worry. She's still here.

112 *Rebecca comes down with her guitar. She sees Sandy.*

113 REBECCA Hey!

114 *The two hug each other.*

115 SANDY Oh, I couldn't let you go without saying one last goodbye . . . and to give you this . . .

116 REBECCA Ah, yes, the mystery present.

117 *Sandy hands her the package. Rebecca opens it. It is a diary. Rebecca is delighted.*

118 REBECCA Oh, Sandy, a diary! It's perfect!

119 SANDY I want you to write down all the good stuff—

120 REBECCA What about the bad stuff?

121 SANDY Oh, absolutely! I want it all in writing. And remember, since I gave you the diary,
122 I get to read it.

123 REBECCA Over my dead body!

124 **KEVIN**   Hey . . . I have something for you, too. (*He hands Rebecca a four-leaf clover key ring.*)

125 **REBECCA**   Kev . . .

126 **KEVIN**   See . . . a little something for good luck. (*Rebecca takes it and laughs.*)

127 **REBECCA**   A four-leaf clover! I love it . . .

128 **KEVIN**   It's a key ring for your new car.

129 **REBECCA**   Thanks, Kev . . . I guess it's that time. (*She gives him a big hug.*)

130 **KEVIN**   I'll see you, Sis. Don't get lost.

131 **REBECCA**   (*holding her diary*) I'll try not to.

132 **SANDY**   I can't believe you're going!

133 **REBECCA**   I know . . .

134 *They give each other a big hug.*

135 **REBECCA**   Well . . .

136 **DAD**   Well, call us tonight . . . and tell us how you are.

137 **REBECCA**   I will.

138 **DAD**   And . . . have a good trip, Becky. Don't worry about us. Just be careful.

139 *Then Rebecca goes to Dad and they hug. She kisses him goodbye.*

140 **KEVIN**   Your guitar.

141 **REBECCA**   Oh, put it in the back seat.

142 **SANDY**   Remember, don't pick up any hitchhikers . . . except for the cute ones!

143 *Rebecca gets in the car. Dad, Kevin, and Sandy watch. She says bye and starts the car.*

144 **SANDY**   Bye . . .

145 **KEVIN**   Bye, Rebecca.

146 **SANDY**   . . . Be careful . . . Bye! (*There is a sad feeling.*)

147 *Rebecca's car drives slowly into a cemetery. Rebecca's car slowly pulls to a stop. She gets out of the car and*
148 *walks to her mother's grave. We see the name "Margaret Casey" on a gravestone.*

149 **REBECCA**   Well, this is it, Mom. I'm off to San Francisco. I'll try and do my very best. Keep
150   an eye on Kevin and Dad for me, hm? I miss you, Mom. Bye.

EPISODE 8

The Stranger

PART 1

1 *ON THE ROAD—DAY*

2 *We see Rebecca's diary and scenes of her trip as she describes them.*

3 **REBECCA**   Day one: I am driving across the United States. I'm leaving the East Coast
4   driving west for new sights, new adventures.

5   Day two: I drove all day through the Midwest.

6   Day three: I crossed over the Mississippi and into the plains.

7 *We hear Rebecca singing with the radio. There is nothing but open spaces—the American Southwest.*

8 **REBECCA**   This is the fourth day of my drive across the United States. It's the desert. The
9   land is flat and barren, but beautiful, in a strange way. The music on the radio out
10   here sure is different from Boston. I'm really starting to like this Tex-Mex music.
11   (*Music plays.*) The car has been pretty good so far, but it's a gas guzzler. I have to
12   fill it up a lot.

13 *GAS STATION*

14 *Rebecca's car heads down a road and pulls into a gas station. A gas attendant approaches wiping his hands.*

15 **GAS ATTENDANT**   Hi. What can I do for you?

16 **REBECCA**   Boy, it's a hot one.

17 **GAS ATTENDANT**   Yeah, and I hear it's gonna get hotter . . . Fill it up?

18 **REBECCA**   Yeah, please. Uh, regular, unleaded . . . Oh, and can you check the oil? Do you
19   have a restroom?

20 **GAS ATTENDANT**   Yup. It's around the corner. The key's inside.

21 *She goes to the office to look for the key. The attendant heads toward the hood.*

22 **REBECCA**   (*calling back*) Excuse me. Where's the key?

23 **GAS ATTENDANT**   It's hanging near the door.

24 *Rebecca walks inside, searches, but can't find it. She steps out and calls out to the attendant.*

25 **REBECCA**   I don't see it.

26 **GAS ATTENDANT**   On the hook . . . by the phone.

27 *She finds the key and heads to the restroom.* ·

28 *AT THE GAS PUMP*

29 *The cash meter on the gas pump goes up and up. Rebecca returns to her car.*

30 **GAS ATTENDANT**   I put in two quarts of oil.

31 **REBECCA**   Two quarts? (*This seems strange to her.*) Why so much?

32 **GAS ATTENDANT**   I don't know. Maybe there's a problem.

33 **REBECCA**   Do you really think there's a problem?

34 **GAS ATTENDANT**   I can't tell. I'm not a mechanic. But the owner, he'll be back in about an
35   hour. He's a mechanic. You should check with him.

36 **REBECCA**   Do you think I should wait?

37 **GAS ATTENDANT**   It's up to you.

38 **REBECCA**   Maybe I'll go on . . . How much do I owe you?

39 **GAS ATTENDANT**   That'll be fifteen seventy-five for the gas . . . plus the oil . . . eighteen
40   ninety. Cash or credit card?

41 **REBECCA**   Cash.

42 *She gives him a twenty and he gives her change. She gets into the car.*

43 **GAS ATTENDANT** You drove all the way from Massachusetts by yourself?

44 **REBECCA** Yup.

45 **GAS ATTENDANT** That's a heck of a drive. How far are you going?

46 **REBECCA** San Francisco. (*The attendant whistles in reply.*)

47 **GAS ATTENDANT** Keep your eye on that oil, OK?

48 **REBECCA** I will. Thanks.

49 **GAS ATTENDANT** Good luck! (*She waves and drives off.*)

50 *The sun is setting in the desert. Rebecca's hair is blowing, but she's looking sweaty and tired.*

51 **REBECCA** Where am I going to sleep tonight? I hope I can find a cheap motel out here.
52   Maybe there's something down this road?

53 *DUSTY ROAD NEAR MOTEL—AFTERNOON*

54 *We see a "Sundowner Motel" sign.*

55 **REBECCA** The Sundowner Motel. Great . . . Oh, no. It's out of business . . . (*looking at map*)
56   Oh, great . . . San Francisco is still 500 miles away. Heck, I'll drive straight
57   through. No more motels. I'm just gonna get there.

PART 2

58 *ON THE ROAD*

59 *Rebecca is driving along when her car makes a noise and stops.*

60 **REBECCA** Oh, don't tell me . . . Now what am I gonna do?

61 *She's starting to get a little panicked. In the distance a man approaches. The sun is behind his back. He is*
62 *wearing a cowboy hat. He carries a long, dark object.*

63 *At first, Rebecca thinks maybe this is help. But then she thinks again. He might be trouble. She tries the car*
64 *again. She rolls up her windows and locks the doors. The man gets closer. She sinks down in the seat a bit.*
65 *He is next to the car. He can see the windows are closed. He looks in.*

66 **ALBERTO** Hi.

67 *Rebecca does nothing—just sits there. Alberto thinks that she can't hear him, so he tries again louder.*

68 **ALBERTO** Hi-eee!

69 *Rebecca continues to ignore him.*

70 **ALBERTO** Hel-lo.

71 *Rebecca gives him a quick look. She sees that he's carrying a camera and tripod, but she still looks straight*
72 *ahead. She tries to start the car, but it won't start up. She tries again.*

73 **ALBERTO** (*shouting*) Do you want to roll down your window?

74 *She tries to start the car, but it doesn't work.*

75 **ALBERTO** (*motioning to the hood*) Car trouble, huh? Look, don't worry about me. I was just
76   taking pictures . . . over there. Well, why don't you pop open the hood, and I'll
77   check it out, OK?

78 *He walks to the front of the car and puts down his camera and tripod. He points to the hood. She releases*
79 *the hood. He disappears under the hood.*

80 **ALBERTO**   *(He calls out and waves.)* OK. Try it now. *(Rebecca tries the car.)* OK, start it up.

81 *Rebecca tries once more to start the engine. Alberto reaches for something in the engine. Rebecca tries again.*
82 *Alberto lets go of the hood, and it falls on him. We hear a yell. We see his startled look and Rebecca's*
83 *frightened face.*

84 *He slowly pushes the hood open again. Rebecca gets out of the car and comes toward him. She is a little bit*
85 *frightened.*

86 **REBECCA**   Are you all right?

87 *Alberto holds his head. He's in pain.*

88 **REBECCA**   Oh, my God, I am so sorry.

89 *He sits on the front fender and holds his head.*

90 **REBECCA**   Do you want to sit down? Look, I'm so . . . oh, God, I'm sorry. Let me see. It's not
91   bleeding . . .

92 *Alberto looks as if he is in pain.*

93 **ALBERTO**   It's, it's not your fault. It's OK.

94 **REBECCA**   I know it's not my fault, but it's my car and I feel terrible. I should get this hood
95   fixed.

96 **ALBERTO**   Yeah, that's a good idea . . . Look, look, I'm sorry I scared you.

97 **REBECCA**   Oh . . . it's OK. It's just with all the stories you hear, you have to be careful.

98 *They look at each other with sympathy and relax a bit.*

99 **ALBERTO**   So, should we try your car one more time?

100 **REBECCA**   Yeah.

101 *Rebecca nods and turns and gets in. Alberto carefully lifts the hood again, making sure it will stay up.*

102 **ALBERTO**   OK, start it up.

103 *Rebecca turns the key. The engine turns over, but it won't catch. Alberto tries to fix it, but he can't.*
104 *Rebecca gets out again.*

105 **ALBERTO**   I'm afraid I don't know what's wrong with your car. It's not getting any gas. It may
106   be the fuel pump. *(He sees that her license plate is from Massachusetts.)*

107 **REBECCA**   Well . . . now what am I going to do?

108 **ALBERTO**   I see you're from Massachusetts. Boston?

109 **REBECCA**   Mm-hmm.

110 **ALBERTO**   Where are you going?

111 **REBECCA**   I'm not going anywhere until I get my car fixed.

112 **ALBERTO**   OK, well, why don't we take my car and . . . uh, we'll try to find a gas station or
113   at least a pay phone.

114 **REBECCA**   Maybe you could go . . . and I'll . . . uh, just stay here with my car.

115 **ALBERTO**   *(noticing the coming sunset)* That's not a good idea. It's late, and everything's going to
116   close soon.

117 **REBECCA**   Well, there has to be a twenty-four-hour place.

118 **ALBERTO**   This isn't Boston. Things pretty much close at sundown.

119 REBECCA   Well, there's got to be a place around here somewhere.

120 ALBERTO   Hey, shh. We're in the middle of nowhere. You may have to wait until morning.

121 REBECCA   (looking concerned) Oh, I don't, I don't . . . (thinks) I guess I don't have much
122   choice.

123 ALBERTO   So, you should take anything that's valuable. I think your car will be safe, but you
124   never know . . .

125 *She goes over and pulls out a few essentials, namely her guitar and purse. She locks the car up. He lowers*
126 *the hood of the car.*

127 **ALBERTO**   (pointing) My car's just up the road there.

128 *ALBERTO'S CAR—EVENING*

129 *Rebecca and Alberto are now walking to his car.*

130 **ALBERTO**   My name's Alberto . . .

131 REBECCA   Mine's Rebecca.

132 **ALBERTO**   Nice to meet you.

133 REBECCA   Nice to meet you, too. (She looks at his camera equipment.) Are you a photographer?

134 **ALBERTO**   No, actually I'm an architect. Photography's just my hobby.

135 REBECCA   Oh . . . What do you take pictures of?

136 **ALBERTO**   Desert, sunsets, shadows . . . light.

137 *He's moving too fast and his head hurts again.*

138 **ALBERTO**   Ow.

139 REBECCA   What is it? Are you OK?

140 **ALBERTO**   I'm fine.

141 *They arrive at his four-wheel-drive car.*

142 REBECCA   Oh, I can drive if you're not feeling well.

143 **ALBERTO**   Really, really—I'm fine.

144 *They get in.*

PART 3

145 *ALBERTO'S CAR—NIGHT*

146 ALBERTO   Do you want me to turn the heat on? The desert gets cold at night.

147 REBECCA   Oh, no, I'm fine. Do you have any idea where we are?

148 ALBERTO   Yeah, Mount Eagle Road. What's that over there?

149 REBECCA   Looks like a hamburger stand or something. Maybe I could make a phone call
150   from there.

151 *ROADSIDE RESTAURANT*

152 *Alberto's car pulls up to a small roadside hamburger stand. The two get out of the car and walk over just as*
153 *the lights are going out. They shout into the stand.*

154 **ALBERTO** Hello! . . . Yo . . . Hey . . .

155 **REBECCA** Hello. We need a phone . . . We, we have car trouble . . .

156 **ALBERTO** There she goes . . .

157 **REBECCA** Ow . . . Hel . . .

158 *The last light goes out. They look at each other.*

159 **REBECCA** Great! Now what?

EPISODE

9

The Motel

PART 1

1 *REBECCA'S DIARY*

2 **REBECCA** Day four: What a night! My car broke down.

3 *ROADSIDE RESTAURANT—NIGHT*

4 *Alberto's car sits next to a small roadside hamburger stand. Rebecca and Alberto arrive just as the restaurant*
5 *lights go out. Rebecca shouts again into the dark hamburger stand.*

6 **ALBERTO** Hello! . . . Yo . . . hey . . .

7 **REBECCA** *(shouting)* Hello, we need a phone . . . We, we have car trouble.

8 **ALBERTO** There she goes . . .

9 **REBECCA** Ow . . . Hel . . .

10 *The last light goes out. They look at each other. Silence from the hamburger stand.*

11 **REBECCA** Great . . . now what?

12 *The lights go on, and out of the side door comes a woman, the owner and chef of this out-of-the-way*
13 *hamburger stand.*

14 **REBECCA** Excuse me, we need a phone. We're having car trouble . . .

15 **RESTAURANT WORKER** We're closed.

16 **REBECCA** We realize that, but it'll only take a few minutes.

17 **RESTAURANT WORKER** What is the problem?

18 **REBECCA** I need to call a mechanic . . . Do you know of any around here?

19 **RESTAURANT WORKER** Joe's Auto Repair—it's the closest.

20 **REBECCA** Oh, well, do you have the phone number by any chance?

21 **RESTAURANT WORKER** For Pete's sake . . . Just a second.

22 *The restaurant worker looks at Rebecca and then at Alberto. She goes back inside.*

23 **REBECCA** Do you think anybody will be at Joe's Garage?

24 **ALBERTO** Let's just take it one step at a time, OK?

25 *The restaurant worker returns with the number on a piece of paper.*

26 **RESTAURANT WORKER** Here it is, Joe's Auto Repair.

27 **REBECCA** Um, could I use your phone?

28 *The restaurant worker looks at Rebecca and Alberto with suspicion.*

29 **RESTAURANT WORKER** OK, make it snappy, though. Go around back. Phone's on the wall.

30 *Rebecca walks around the back and enters the hamburger stand. Alberto and the restaurant worker wait*
31 *outside the hamburger stand.*

32 **ALBERTO** Hi. Listen, is there a chance that maybe I could get something to eat before
33   you close?

34 **RESTAURANT WORKER** *(shaking her head)* No. Grill's turned off.

35 *Alberto is having a bad day. Now, he can't even get a bite to eat. He and the restaurant worker*
36 *wait outside.*

37 **ALBERTO** *(making small talk)* Sure is windy, huh?

38 **RESTAURANT WORKER** It's always windy out here . . . God . . . *(to Rebecca)* Did you find the
39   phone yet?

40 *The restaurant worker and Alberto go through the side door. They look in. Rebecca is on the phone. Alberto*
41 *and the restaurant worker watch from the doorway. Rebecca is interrupted by a recorded message.*

42 **REBECCA** Yes, but I'm not getting any . . . Oh, it's ringing . . . *(sigh)* Oh, no, it's an
43   answering machine.

44 **JOE** You've reached Joe's Auto Repair. We're open from seven to four, Monday
45   through Friday. If this is an emergency, please leave a short message including the
46   location of your car. Thank you for calling. *(His voice stops and a tone sounds.)*

47 **REBECCA** *(talking to machine)* This is Rebecca Casey. My car broke down in . . . *(to restaurant*
48   *worker and Alberto)* Where are we?

49 **RESTAURANT WORKER** You're in Iron Mount . . . Jessie's Hamburger Stand.

50 **REBECCA** In Iron Mount . . . I-it's near the, uh . . . the Sundowner Motel. It's a gray Delta
51   eighty-eight Oldsmobile . . . with Massachusetts license plates. Would you please
52   send a tow truck? . . . *(to restaurant worker and Alberto)* Nobody was there. I got an
53   answering machine. Do you think that Joe will get the message tonight?

54 **RESTAURANT WORKER** I don't know if Joe picks up his messages at night or not. Your best
55   bet's just to call him back in the morning.

56 **ALBERTO** She's right. *(Rebecca thinks for a second and then comes to a conclusion.)*

57 **REBECCA** Hm . . . Guess I'll need a place to stay tonight. Are there any motels around here?

58 **RESTAURANT WORKER** Only place that's open out here is the Starlight Lodge. Follow me, I
59   go right by it.

PART 2

60 *ROAD NEAR MOTEL—NIGHT*

61 *The restaurant worker sticks her arm out the window of her truck and points toward a motel.*

62 *PARKING LOT—Slowly, Alberto's car drives through the parking lot. There are big trucks everywhere.*

63 **REBECCA** Lots of trucks. I hope they have a room.

64 **ALBERTO** Yeah.

65 *MOTEL PARKING LOT*

66 *Rebecca notices Alberto taking out his own suitcase.*

67 **REBECCA** What are you doing?

68 **ALBERTO** Gettin' my suitcase.

69 **REBECCA** Are you gonna stay here, too?

70 **ALBERTO** Where else am I gonna stay?

71 *He closes his trunk and heads into the motel. Rebecca follows.*

72 **ALBERTO** Let's get outta the rain, huh?

73 *MOTEL*

74 *The clerk is playing with a lottery card. It is the kind that you scratch to see if you've won a prize.*
75 *Rebecca and Alberto enter the motel reception room.*

76 **ALBERTO** How ya doin'?

77 **CLERK** Hello. Just one second please . . . Scratch card. Today could be my lucky day!
78 (*He scratches the card.*) Never any good luck here when it rains.

79 **REBECCA** Do you have any rooms available?

80 **CLERK** Hey, you're the lucky couple. I just had a cancellation. You and the Mrs. can
81 have that room. Thirty-nine, ninety-five a night. In advance.

82 **REBECCA** You don't understand. We're not together . . . I mean, we're not a couple. That's
83 why I said 'rooms,' because we need two rooms.

84 **CLERK** You're not a couple?

85 *The clerk looks at Alberto. Alberto shakes his head "no." The clerk wonders why they're together.*

86 **REBECCA** No. Is there another room available?

87 **CLERK** (*shaking his head*) No, sorry.

88 **ALBERTO** You go and take the room.

89 **REBECCA** No, I am not gonna do this.

90 **ALBERTO** Are there any other motels near here?

91 **CLERK** The closest one is an hour-and-a-half south.

92 **ALBERTO** Well, I'm headed north. How 'bout north of here?

93 **CLERK** Nothing closer than two hours. (*Alberto is surprised.*)

94 **ALBERTO** One minute . . . (*turns to Rebecca*) Um . . . I'll sleep in my car.

95 **REBECCA** No, I don't—

96 **ALBERTO** Hey, it's not the first time . . .

97 *The clerk listens to them closely.*

98 **REBECCA** No, but it's not right . . .

99 **ALBERTO** I'll be fine . . .

100	REBECCA	Why don't I just sleep in the car?
101	ALBERTO	No way . . .
102	REBECCA	I don't want to give you any more trouble.
103	ALBERTO	It's out of the question.
104	REBECCA	Really, I can sleep in the car—
105 ALBERTO		*(laughing)* All right, enough of this! Enough of this. Look, look, it's my car, I've
106		slept in it before . . . I'll sleep in it again.
107	REBECCA	Are you sure?
108	ALBERTO	Absolutely sure.
109	REBECCA	Thanks.
110	ALBERTO	She'll take the room. *(The clerk points to the registration book.)*
111	CLERK	You'll need to register. If you'll just fill this out, please.
112	REBECCA	Mm-hm. Oh, do you take credit cards?
113 CLERK		We take plastic, travelers' checks, dollars, pesos, whatever, as long as you have a
114		driver's license.
115	REBECCA	That, I have.

116 *Rebecca looks for and places her license on the counter. She then begins to fill out the registration card.*

117	ALBERTO	Do you serve food?
118	CLERK	Sorry, all we have is a candy machine.

119 *The clerk hands her a room key, a small paper bath mat, a towel, and a very small bar of soap.*
120 *Both Rebecca and Alberto look at the small towel with some surprise.*

121	REBECCA	Um . . . Do you have anything larger? I'd like to dry both hands tonight.
122 CLERK		*(He hands her a few more.)* Here, sorry . . . take some more. I know they're kind
123		of tiny.

124 *Rebecca and Alberto laugh as she takes more towels.*

125	CLERK	And you are in room four.
126	REBECCA	Great.
127	ALBERTO	*(to the clerk)* Thanks.

128 *OUTSIDE THE MOTEL*

129	REBECCA	Two . . . Three . . . here it is, four. *(They stop at her door.)*
130	ALBERTO	You gonna be all right here?
131	REBECCA	I think so. Let me take a look at the room. *(She opens the door.)*
132	REBECCA	Oh, where's the light switch?
133	ALBERTO	Here, I'll get it.

134 *INSIDE THE MOTEL ROOM*

135 *Rebecca and Alberto walk into the room.*

136 **ALBERTO** It's not too bad.

137 **REBECCA** It's not the Ritz, but it'll be fine.

138 **ALBERTO** Can I borrow a blanket?

139 **REBECCA** Oh, of course. (*She walks towards the blanket on the shelf.*)

140 **ALBERTO** It's gonna make that car a little more comfortable, ya know.

141 *Rebecca hands Alberto the blanket.*

142 **REBECCA** By the way, how's your head? Every time I think about that car hood falling on
143   your head . . .

144 **ALBERTO** Don't remind me . . . Do you have an aspirin?

145 **REBECCA** (*Looking in her bag, she finds a bottle of aspirin, and gives it to Alberto.*) Uh . . . Right here.

146 *Both are unsure of what to do or say next.*

147 **ALBERTO** And . . . I'll probably need a glass of water.

148 **REBECCA** Oh, sure . . . Sorry.

149 *She looks for a glass. She finds one wrapped in plastic and opens it.*

150 **REBECCA** Plastic . . . (*turning around*) Oh, water.

151 *She fills the glass and gives him the water.*

152 **REBECCA** There.

153 **ALBERTO** Thanks. (*He takes the aspirin and drinks the water.*)

154 **REBECCA** Thanks for everything. And I'm gonna get up early tomorrow and call the garage
155   about my car.

156 **ALBERTO** That's probably a good idea . . . Well, thanks and, goodnight. I, uh, I'll see you in
157   the morning.

158 *He picks up the blanket and begins to go.*

159 **REBECCA** Thanks for all your help.

160 **ALBERTO** Yeah . . . No problem . . . Bag.

161 *He gets his bag and heads out the door.*

162 *OUTSIDE THE MOTEL*

163 *Alberto walks to his car, the blanket under one arm, his suitcase under the other. Rebecca looks after him.*

PART 3

164 *OUTSIDE THE MOTEL—NIGHT*

165 *Alberto walks back to his car. He opens the door and starts to put his suitcase in. He realizes this is not*
166 *going to be a comfortable night's sleep.*

167 **ALBERTO** (*talking to himself*) . . . car. I can't believe I got myself into this . . . (*sigh*)

168 *Alberto tries to get comfortable but he's too big for the back seat. There is a loud truck noise. He sits up and*
169 *looks out.*

170 **ALBERTO** Huh-huh-oh, now what?

171 *A big, sixteen-wheel truck pulls in right next to his car. It makes a very loud noise as it stops. Alberto tries*
172 *to ignore the truck next to him. However, the noises from the truck keep him awake. The trucker gets down*
173 *from his cabin and leaves the motor running. The trucker drops a wrench. Alberto rolls down his window.*
174 *The trucker is working. Alberto sticks his head out and tries to call to the trucker, but the noise is too loud.*

175 **ALBERTO**   Buddy . . . Excuse me!

176 *The trucker turns around. He is surprised to find someone in the car.*

177 **TRUCKER**   What the . . . *(He moves closer to Alberto.)* Whatta you doin' out here?

178 **ALBERTO**   Do you mind keeping it down?

179 **TRUCKER**   What?

180 **ALBERTO**   I'm trying to sleep.

181 **TRUCKER**   Why don't you pay for a room like everybody else?

182 **ALBERTO**   Don't you think I already tried that? There aren't any more rooms!

183 **TRUCKER**   Well, I have to fix this truck. If I don't, I lose a day's pay.

184 *The trucker returns to his repairs. Alberto pulls back into the car. Alberto can't stand the noise anymore.*
185 *He leans out the window again.*

186 **ALBERTO**   Hey! How long is this gonna take?

187 **TRUCKER**   How the hell should I know?

188 **ALBERTO**   Can't it wait till morning?

189 *The trucker walks over to Alberto's car.*

190 **TRUCKER**   Hey, buddy, this is a free country, ya know. I can do whatever I want, whenever I
191   want. If you don't like it, move!

192 **ALBERTO**   I can't believe this . . .

193 *Alberto gets out of the car and walks around to the driver's seat.*

194 *INSIDE THE MOTEL*

195 *Rebecca grabs a pillow and takes it to give to Alberto.*

196 *OUTSIDE THE MOTEL*

197 *With the pillow under her arm, Rebecca walks toward the noisy truck and driver. She looks for Alberto's car,*
198 *but it's gone.*

199 **REBECCA**   Alberto!

200 *Suddenly, the trucker turns around and looks at her.*

201 **TRUCKER**   Uh . . . ma'am, how ya doin'?

202 *Rebecca looks at him. She is afraid and runs back into her motel room. The trucker looks at her and*
203 *wonders what's going on.*

Negotiations

PART 1

1 *REBECCA'S DIARY*

2 **REBECCA** Day five: Morning comes to the desert. The rain has stopped.

3 *REBECCA'S MOTEL ROOM—MORNING*

4 *Rebecca is dressed and ready for the new day's adventure. Rebecca dials Joe's Auto Repair and waits for*
5 *someone to answer the phone.*

6 *INSIDE JOE'S AUTO REPAIR*

7 **JOE** Joe's Auto Repair. This is Joe speaking. What can I do for ya?

8 **REBECCA** This is Rebecca Casey. Listen, I left you a message last night about my car . . .

9 **JOE** It's sittin' right here.

10 **REBECCA** Great! Do you know what the problem is?

11 **JOE** Not yet. It'll take a coupla hours.

12 **REBECCA** A couple of hours! I have a long trip ahead of me.

13 **JOE** I just got it in. Call me back in a couple of hours.

14 **REBECCA** *(sighs)* I'll call back in two hours, is that OK?

15 **JOE** All right.

16 *Rebecca gets up and gathers her belongings. There's a knock on the door.*

17 **REBECCA** Who is it?

18 **ALBERTO** It's Alberto.

19 **REBECCA** Oh, c'mon in!

20 *Alberto opens the door, a blanket in his hand. He's slightly bent over—his back hurts from sleeping*
21 *in the car.*

22 **REBECCA** Hey, you're still here! I went to bring you a pillow last night. I thought you'd left.

23 **ALBERTO** Oh really? Oh, man, I'm sorry. A trucker came up and pulled next to me . . . and
24 he was makin' too much noise, so I went on the other side of the motel.

25 **REBECCA** I'm glad you didn't leave.

26 **ALBERTO** Um . . . may I ask you a favor?

27 **REBECCA** Of course.

28 **ALBERTO** Can I use your shower?

29 **REBECCA** Oh, yeah, sure!

30 **ALBERTO** My back's really stiff and I think a hot shower would . . .

31 *Alberto heads toward the bathroom.*

32	REBECCA	Yeah, go right ahead. Um . . . (*hands him a little towel*) All the other towels are wet.
33		This is the only one that's dry. Sorry.
34	ALBERTO	That's fine. (*The conversation continues as Alberto closes the door.*)
35	REBECCA	(*to herself, as she checks her belongings*) OK . . .
36	ALBERTO	So, what's happening with your car?
37	REBECCA	Oh, it's at Joe's Auto Repair.
38	ALBERTO	Really. Does he know what's wrong with it?
39	REBECCA	No, not yet. I have to call back in two hours.
40	ALBERTO	Oh. Ya know, you should be careful. Sometimes those mechanics don't know
41		what they're doin'.
42	REBECCA	Yeah, but I'm at his mercy. (*Rebecca quickly finishes gathering up her possessions.*) Listen,
43		uh . . . I don't want to bother you anymore. So I'm just going to take a taxi over
44		to the garage . . . (*yelling into the door*) Thank you for everything
45		yesterday . . .

46 *Suddenly the door opens, and Alberto sticks out his wet head and shoulders.*

47	ALBERTO	Hey, I was . . . I was glad to help. You, you don't have to take a taxi . . . I'll drive
48		you over there. Just wait till I'm done showering . . .
49	REBECCA	Oh, it's really not necessary. Thank you, again. Bye.

50 *She turns and quickly leaves the motel room with her guitar and purse. Alberto looks puzzled. Rebecca closes*
51 *the door behind her and walks toward the lobby.*

52 MOTEL LOBBY

53 *Rebecca enters and walks to the desk where the clerk is listening to music on headphones. His head is moving*
54 *to the music. Rebecca tries to get his attention.*

| 55 | REBECCA | Excuse me. (*No response.*) Excuse me . . . hello. |

56 *When she still gets no response, she leans over the desk and taps his shoulder. He sees it's a guest of the*
57 *motel. He smiles and removes his headphones. The clerk now turns his attention to Rebecca.*

58	CLERK	I'm sorry. How are you today, ma'am?
59	REBECCA	Fine, thank you. I need to get a taxi as soon as possible.
60	CLERK	A taxi?
61	REBECCA	I need to go over to Joe's Auto Repair.
62	CLERK	The nearest taxi is in Indio, at least an hour away.
63	REBECCA	Oh, come on.
64	CLERK	Honest.
65	REBECCA	Well, how can I get over to the garage?
66	CLERK	Why don't you thumb a ride with one of our truckers? (*He demonstrates in a*
67		*funny way.*)
68	REBECCA	Hitchhike?
69	CLERK	Well sure. I'll . . . ask around. See who's going . . .

70 **REBECCA**   No, I don't think so. I, I don't think that it's safe . . . but thanks, anyway.

71 **CLERK**   *(shrugs)* Well, suit yourself . . . um . . .What about your friend—the guy who slept
72   in the car?

73 *MOTEL PARKING LOT*

74 *Alberto loads his suitcase into the car. Rebecca walks up to Alberto.*

75 **REBECCA**   Um . . . *(sigh)*

76 **ALBERTO**   Hey.

77 **REBECCA**   Hey.

78 **ALBERTO**   Still here, huh? Where's your taxi?

79 **REBECCA**   Uh . . . This, this is embarrassing . . . But I tried to get a taxi over to the garage
80   and there aren't any. And I hate to ask, but . . . could you drop me off there?

81 **ALBERTO**   *(making her uncomfortable just a bit)* I don't know, Rebecca . . .

82 **REBECCA**   *(sigh)* All right—

83 **ALBERTO**   *(He looks up smiling.)* Sure. I'd be happy to take you.

PART 2

84 *DESERT CENTER CAFE*

85 *Alberto's car pulls into a parking lot.*

86 **ALBERTO**   Look, I'm starving. Let's get a bite to eat, OK?

87 **REBECCA**   Well . . . we should go over there, don't you think?

88 **ALBERTO**   *(interrupting)* The garage said two hours, right?

89 **REBECCA**   Yeah, I guess there's no rush.

90 *DESERT CENTER CAFE SIGN*

91 *Alberto parks the car, and he and Rebecca get out.*

92 **REBECCA**   Desert . . . Center Cafe?

93 **ALBERTO**   We don't have a choice. I don't know about you, but I need to eat. I'm starving.
94   Aren't you hungry?

95 **REBECCA**   Yeah, I guess so . . . Yeah, I'm pretty hungry.

96 *Alberto and Rebecca are sitting at the counter. Plates of eggs and fries are placed in front of our two*
97 *travelers. They smile and begin to eat.*

98 **ALBERTO**   *(taking a bite of food)* So, where exactly are you going?

99 **REBECCA**   California. San Francisco.

100 **ALBERTO**   You're kidding.

101 **REBECCA**   No. Why do you think I'm kidding?

102 **ALBERTO**   Because I'm from San Francisco. That's where I live.

103 **REBECCA**   Really? What a coincidence.

104 **ALBERTO**   Isn't it?

105 **REBECCA** Small world . . .

106 **ALBERTO** So what are you going to do in San Francisco?

107 **REBECCA** I got accepted to the San Francisco College of Music.

108 **ALBERTO** Oh. And what do you wanna do when you finish music school?

109 **REBECCA** Well, I hope to be a songwriter.

110 **ALBERTO** What kinda songs do you write?

111 **REBECCA** Folk and pop, with a little jazz influence.

112 **ALBERTO** I can't believe you're moving to San Francisco.

113 **REBECCA** I know. (*Rebecca sips her coffee.*)

114 *CASHIER*

115 *Alberto pays the check. As the clerk makes change, they see several dream catchers hanging on a rack beside*
116 *the cash register. Rebecca picks one up.*

117 **REBECCA** Alberto, do you know what this is?

118 **ALBERTO** That is a dream catcher.

119 **REBECCA** What's a 'dream catcher'?

120 **ALBERTO** Well, according to Native American legend, if you place a dream catcher over
121 your bed at night, it catches all the bad dreams . . . and it lets in only the good
122 ones.

123 **REBECCA** How wonderful. We all need a dream catcher in our lives.

PART 3

124 *INSIDE JOE'S AUTO REPAIR—DAY*

125 *Joe is adding up Rebecca's bill on an old calculator.*

126 **JOE** Let's see . . . parts . . . labor . . . and, oh yeah, there's the towing . . .

127 **REBECCA** I had hoped to be on my way to San Francisco by now. God, this feels like a bad
128 dream . . .

129 **ALBERTO** Yeah, where's a dream catcher when you need one?

130 **JOE** Well, we have two problems: first, I need your OK on this before I can go ahead
131 with the work (*shoves the estimate in front of her*) . . . Sign right here . . . And,
132 second, I have the fuel pump, I think . . . Excuse me . . .

133 **ALBERTO** Sorry.

134 *Joe exits for a moment. Alberto can tell that Rebecca is worried.*

135 **ALBERTO** (*softly to Rebecca*) Calm down . . . (*Joe returns with the fuel pump.*)

136 **JOE** Got it right here. But I don't have the right gasket. I'll have to send out for one.

137 **REBECCA** Send out! Where?

138 **JOE** Well, I usually get my parts from a place in Mason, but . . .

139 **REBECCA** How long will that take?

140	JOE	I was about to say . . . but it'll take at least a day or two, and that's if they have
141		what I need.
142	REBECCA	And what'll the whole thing cost?
143	JOE	Well, lemme check the price of the gasket . . . Lemme see . . . around five
144		hundred and twenty dollars . . .
145	REBECCA	Oh, no.
146	JOE	And I noticed there's a problem with the steering . . . tie rods, I'm afraid.
147	REBECCA	Well, is it something that can wait? I mean, can I—can I wait till I get to
148		San Francisco?
149	ALBERTO	You shouldn't take a chance with your steering.

150 *Rebecca looks at Alberto, and then she looks back at Joe.*

151	JOE	He's right.
152	REBECCA	And how much will that cost?
153	JOE	Off the top of my head . . . another two hundred fifty to three hundred.

154 *Rebecca is not certain what to do.*

155	REBECCA	I—I need to think about this. (*She heads outside. Alberto follows her.*)
156	ALBERTO	You want my advice? . . . Let him fix it.
157	REBECCA	I need to think about this. Gimme a few minutes.

158 *She steps out. Joe joins Alberto, who is watching Rebecca pacing and thinking.*

159	JOE	How long will it take your girlfriend to make up her mind?
160	ALBERTO	She's—she's not my girlfriend. She's just a friend, and I'm sure she'll make a
161		decision quickly.

162 *Rebecca again approaches Joe, who is now writing up an estimate on the work needed. He turns to her.*

163	JOE	So, what do ya wanna do?
164	REBECCA	I don't have eight hundred dollars to spend on that car. I have to sell it. Is there
165		any chance that you would buy it from me?
166	JOE	Buy your car?
167	ALBERTO	Yeah, how are you gonna get back to . . . ?
168	REBECCA	With the money, I can take a bus to San Francisco. (*to Joe*) It's not a bad car. I
169		mean, my father paid a lot of money for that car a few weeks ago. I'm sure you
170		could sell it for a decent price, after you fix it up.
171	JOE	Well, there isn't much demand for cars like that around here. People around here
172		want mostly pickups.
173	REBECCA	I'm sure you could sell it to somebody. Do you wanna make me an offer?
174	JOE	Well . . . I suppose I could sell it for parts . . . I'll give you three hundred . . .
175	REBECCA	Three hundred! It's worth a thousand at least.

176 *Alberto tries not to laugh, shaking his head.*

| 177 | JOE | OK, how about four hundred? |

178	REBECCA	It's yours for seven hundred.
179	JOE	Five is as high as I can go.
180	ALBERTO	You know, it's worth a lot more than that. C'mon.
181		*Joe looks at them; they look at him—who's going to break first?*
182	JOE	Five twenty-five.
183	REBECCA	Five seventy-five.
184	JOE	OK, five-fifty. Lord knows, it's my good deed for the day.
185	REBECCA	Five-fifty. Sold.
186	REBECCA	Now . . . are there any buses to San Francisco around here?
187 188	JOE	Yup. Greyhound bus stops in Indio. Right down Route 10, about a half-hour from here. One bus a day, it leaves at two. (*Rebecca looks at her watch.*)
189	REBECCA	So . . . now, it's eleven o'clock.
190	ALBERTO	Plenty of time to make the bus.
191	REBECCA	Do you mind driving me?
192	ALBERTO	Course not. I'll have you there by two.
193	REBECCA	Thanks . . . I guess I should get all my things out of my car.
194	ALBERTO	Yeah.

195 *LATER THAT DAY*

196 *Alberto and Rebecca are almost done transferring the luggage from Rebecca's car to Alberto's. Joe, having*
197 *taken the plates off of the car, approaches with a receipt.*

198 199	JOE	One last thing—title to the car. You have to sign it over to me. The name's Joe Steward. That's S-T-E-W-A-R-D.

200 *Rebecca takes Joe's pen and signs the receipt. She hands it to Joe. Joe hands her the $550. They shake hands.*

201	JOE	Thank you. One-two-three-four-fifty-five, and fifty. Let's see here . . . Receipt . . .
202	REBECCA	Thanks for everything.
203	JOE	No problem. Here are your plates. (*He shakes Alberto's hand.*)
204	ALBERTO	Yeah . . . thanks. (*Joe hands Alberto a towel to wipe off the grease.*)
205	JOE	Here you go.
206	ALBERTO	So . . . you ready to go?
207	REBECCA	Yeah.

208 *ALBERTO'S CAR*

209 *Alberto is driving.*

210 211	REBECCA	I, I feel really embarrassed . . . You're driving me to my next destination. I, I feel like you've become my taxi driver . . .
212	ALBERTO	If I were a taxi, you couldn't afford me.
213	REBECCA	I don't know how I can ever thank you . . .

214 **ALBERTO** Forget it! Listen, I was thinking . . . We're going to the same place . . . and I
215   didn't think of this before . . .

216 **REBECCA** I beg your pardon?

217 **ALBERTO** We're going to the same place, right?

218 **REBECCA** Yes?

219 **ALBERTO** Well, why don't we ride . . . together?

220 **REBECCA** Oh-uh . . .

221 **ALBERTO** We'll drive straight through . . .

222 **REBECCA** No, I, I appreciate the generous offer, but I don't think so. I think I'd better take
223   a bus.

224 **ALBERTO** C'mon! It makes perfectly—perfectly good sense . . .

225 **REBECCA** Alberto . . . I, I think I should take the bus.

226 **ALBERTO** But, you know, but why spend the money?

227 **REBECCA** The bus. (*He gets the message.*)

228 **ALBERTO** Right, the bus.

Photos and Farewells

PART 1

1 *REBECCA'S DIARY*

2 **REBECCA** Day five. Alberto helped me out, again. My car broke down. I'll have to take a
3   bus to San Francisco.

4 *INSIDE ALBERTO'S CAR—DAY*

5 *Alberto is driving. He looks over at Rebecca.*

6 **ALBERTO** Seriously, though, I mean, we, let me take you back to San Francisco. It's going to
7   be faster and cheaper.

8 **REBECCA** I appreciate the offer . . . but . . . I think I'll take the bus.

9 *Alberto drives for a short while and then decides to ask one more time.*

10 **ALBERTO** Yeah, I suppose you have to be careful . . . You just can't drive with anyone.

11 **REBECCA** But I still don't even know your last name.

12 **ALBERTO** Mendoza. Actually, it's (*with a Spanish accent*) Alberto Manuel Mendoza.

13 **REBECCA** (*surprised*) That's a pretty good Spanish accent.

14 **ALBERTO** My family is from Mexico.

15 **REBECCA** Where in Mexico?

16 **ALBERTO** A little village west of Monterey . . . So, what's your full name?

17	**REBECCA**	Rebecca Mary Theresa Casey. My grandparents are from Ireland.
18	**ALBERTO**	Dublin?
19 20	**REBECCA**	No, from the west . . . It's a little town in Galway. I'm told it's a beautiful place, but it's a very poor town.
21	**ALBERTO**	My family's village was poor, too. You know—no money, no jobs, just politics . . .
22	**REBECCA**	I guess that's why both our families moved to the United States.
23 24	**ALBERTO**	Oh, yeah, that's right . . . to have a better life, to get an education, and to make a living . . .
25	**REBECCA**	Yeah, well, my family never did.
26	**ALBERTO**	Well, hey . . . you'll be the first.
27	**REBECCA**	What do you mean?
28	**ALBERTO**	Come on, you'll write some wonderful pop song and become a huge hit.
29	**REBECCA**	Yeah *(laughing)*. I like the way you think.
30	**ALBERTO**	Me, too.

31 *CANYON AREA*

32 *The car stops and Alberto opens the door and steps out.*

33	**ALBERTO**	Wow, these canyons are spectacular.
34 35	**REBECCA**	Yeah, it, it says here that these canyons were sacred to the Agua Caliente Indians.
36	**ALBERTO**	It's pronounced 'Agua Caliente.'
37	**REBECCA**	*(repeating)* Agua Caliente.
38	**ALBERTO**	Now I've got to take some photos. Do you mind carrying my bag?
39	**REBECCA**	No, not at all.

40 *Rebecca and Alberto explore an area of beautiful canyons. They look at a rock with letters carved into it.*

41	**REBECCA**	It's hard to imagine what these canyons were like so many years ago.
42	**ALBERTO**	Probably much the same as they are today . . . Look at that over there.

43 44 *They walk to an area filled with beautiful palm trees and running water. Alberto is carrying his camera and tripod.*

45	**REBECCA**	This is really amazing. They must call this a desert oasis.
46	**ALBERTO**	Yeah, I bet you these palm trees are over a hundred years old.

47 *Alberto places his tripod.*

48	**ALBERTO**	This is it. Could you do me a favor?
49	**REBECCA**	Umhmm.
50	**ALBERTO**	I, I need someone in this picture. Can you stand over by the palm tree?
51	**REBECCA**	Alberto, there are more interesting things to photograph here than me.
52 53	**ALBERTO**	No really, I'm serious. I, I, I need you in the picture to give the picture a sense of scale.

54 **REBECCA** But, I, I don't know . . .

55 **ALBERTO** Please . . .

56 **REBECCA** Well, since you've gone out of your way, I guess it's the least I can do . . .

57 **ALBERTO** All right, yeah, stand over . . . that palm tree to your right. There, perfect.

58 *Rebecca stands next to a tree. We watch as she moves according to Alberto's directions.*

59 **ALBERTO** Yes. Turn, turn a, yeah, turn around a little bit . . . There, there you go . . . Yes . . .
60 Yes . . . Yes.

61 **REBECCA** What, what time is it!

62 **ALBERTO** You know, you look great on camera. Thank you.

63 **REBECCA** Oh, we have to go. My bus leaves in less than an hour.

64 **ALBERTO** Hold it, hold it, hold it right there. Hold, hold it.

65 **REBECCA** Alberto, please. There is only one bus a day. I have to make it on time.

66 *As she gets very close, he takes another picture.*

67 **ALBERTO** Thanks.

PART 2

68 *INSIDE ALBERTO'S CAR—DAY*

69 *We hear the siren of a police car. Alberto pulls over.*

70 **ALBERTO** Oh, man, a cop.

71 *The officer approaches the driver's side of the car as Alberto rolls down his window.*

72 **OFFICER** Hi. Know how fast you were going?

73 **ALBERTO** Mmm—maybe sixty-five?

74 **OFFICER** Eighty miles an hour. License and registration, please.

75 *Rebecca hands Alberto the registration. He gives the license and registration to the officer.*

76 **ALBERTO** Registration, license.

77 **REBECCA** Officer, let me explain—we were just trying . . .

78 **OFFICER** I'll be right back.

79 *HIGHWAY*

80 *The policeman returns to his car to check on the license and registration.*

81 **REBECCA** I hope he doesn't give you a ticket.

82 **ALBERTO** (*Alberto nods in agreement.*) You can say that again.

83 *The policeman returns to Alberto's car.*

84 **POLICEMAN** OK, since you don't have any points on your license, this time, I'll give you
85 a warning.

86 **ALBERTO** Thank you, officer.

87 **REBECCA** Thanks.

88 *The policeman walks away.*

89 **REBECCA**   Whew! How lucky is that: he didn't give you a ticket.

90 **ALBERTO**   Yes . . . whew.

91 *Alberto's car moves through the desert, keeping just within the speed limit.*

PART 3

92 *BUS STATION—DAY*

93 **ALBERTO**   Oh, hold on. I'll take the luggage. You get the ticket.

94 **REBECCA**   Thank you.

95 **ALBERTO**   You're welcome.

96 **GREYHOUND AGENT**   May I help you?

97 **REBECCA**   *(rushing)* Yeah . . . I need a ticket to San Francisco.

98 **GREYHOUND AGENT**   Round trip?

99 **REBECCA**   I need a one-way ticket to San Francisco.

100 *The Greyhound agent enters the information at his computer terminal.*

101 **GREYHOUND AGENT**   So, what's taking you to San Fran?

102 **REBECCA**   Oh, college and a job.

103 **GREYHOUND AGENT**   Um, people seem to think you can't tie your shoelaces without a
104   college degree these days . . . Um, let's see . . . Um, sixty-five dollars.

105 **REBECCA**   *(surprised)* Sixty-five? Is that one-way or round trip?

106 **GREYHOUND AGENT**   One-way. That's what you asked for.

107 **REBECCA**   Yeah.

108 *Rebecca takes some money out and counts it. Alberto now has everything out of his car. The bus driver is*
109 *loading the bags onto the bus.*

110 **BUS DRIVER**   *(working hard)* Is all this baggage yours?

111 **ALBERTO**   No, it's my friend's.

112 *Rebecca comes out just as the driver picks up the guitar to put it on the bus. Rebecca takes it back quickly.*

113 **REBECCA**   Oh, I can take the guitar on the bus. Thanks for all of your help.

114 **ALBERTO**   My pleasure. *(The driver gives him a look.)* Actually, your driver here did all of
115   the work.

116 **BUS DRIVER**   Where are you going?

117 **REBECCA**   San Francisco.

118 **BUS DRIVER**   Oh, you know, you have to change in L.A.? *(Rebecca nods.)*

119 **REBECCA**   Well, I really appreciate your help.

120 **BUS DRIVER**   Oh, is that it?

121 **REBECCA**   Ah, is that everything out of your car?

122 **ALBERTO**   Yeah.

123 **REBECCA**   Yeah, that's it.

124 **BUS DRIVER**   Your ticket, please.

125 *She hands him the ticket. He goes into the bus depot.*

126 **BUS DRIVER** We're leaving in two minutes.

127 **REBECCA** Guess this is it. Thanks for all your help . . .

128 **ALBERTO** It was wonderful meeting you . . . I mean, all except for the part when the hood
129 of your car fell on my head.

130 **REBECCA** Does your head still hurt?

131 **ALBERTO** No. Not really. I'll never forget that look on your face when I found you in the
132 desert . . .

133 **REBECCA** I'll never forget when you were sleeping in your car.

134 **ALBERTO** And Tom the Trucker with that engine he borrowed from a seven-forty-seven—
135 yeah.

136 **REBECCA** Thanks for being such a good sport.

137 **ALBERTO** You're welcome . . .

138 *The bus driver exits the bus depot.*

139 **BUS DRIVER** All aboard.

140 *Rebecca looks as if she's waiting for Alberto to say more.*

141 **ALBERTO** Rebecca, look, since we'll both be in San Francisco, um, why don't we get
142 together?

143 **REBECCA** Well . . . I, I, I don't think I'll have much free time . . . with school and work
144 and . . .

145 **ALBERTO** You can't study all the time, right? You need to take a break . . . once in a while.

146 **REBECCA** (*Rebecca smiles.*) Yeah.

147 **ALBERTO** I, It'd be my honor to show you the city. Where can I reach you?

148 **REBECCA** I'm staying with my godmother.

149 **ALBERTO** Does she have a name?

150 **REBECCA** Nancy Shaw.

151 **ALBERTO** Do you mind giving me her address and her phone number?

152 **REBECCA** Oh, yeah, I have it somewhere. Wait a second.

153 *Alberto waits as Rebecca looks through her bag.*

154 **REBECCA** Alberto, I need to explain something to you. (*pause*) I had a boyfriend in Boston.
155 We broke up before I left. For, for now, I just want to concentrate on my music
156 and worry about my . . .

157 **ALBERTO** Rebecca, I just wanna show you my hometown.

158 **REBECCA** Thanks.

159 *Rebecca gives him a slip of paper with Nancy Shaw's name and address.*

160 **ALBERTO** Yeah. And listen, um, if you have any spare time, here is my business card. Call
161 me . . .

162 *Rebecca looks at the card. The bus driver appears at the door of the bus.*

163 **BUS DRIVER** OK, folks. We have to go. You two love birds have to say 'goodbye.'

164 *Rebecca leans forward to give Alberto a kiss on the cheek, gathers her bags, and gets on the bus. The bus*
165 *starts to pull out. Alberto waves goodbye. Rebecca gives a little wave. Alberto watches the bus leave.*

166 *HIGHWAY*

167 *We see Alberto's car as it travels along the highway.*

168 *DESERT CENTER CAFE*

169 *Alberto goes to the counter of the cafe. He speaks to the cashier.*

170 **ALBERTO** I'd like this dream catcher, please. (*He holds it up.*)

EPISODE
12

A New Home

PART 1

1 *REBECCA'S DIARY*

2 **REBECCA** Day six: San Francisco, here I come.

3 *SAN FRANCISCO BUS STATION—AFTERNOON*

4 *Rebecca Casey gets off the bus. She looks around. She looks tired from the long ride. Rebecca sees Nancy*
5 *Shaw waiting in the bus terminal.*

6 **REBECCA** Nancy?

7 **NANCY** Rebecca! . . . Is that you?

8 **REBECCA** Yes, it's me . . . Hi, how are you? It's so nice to see you, after all these years.

9 **NANCY** It's good to see you! My, my . . . you certainly look like your mother! (*They hug*
10 *each other.*) Welcome . . . welcome to San Francisco.

11 **REBECCA** It's good to be here. It was a long trip.

12 **NANCY** What exactly happened to your car?

13 **REBECCA** Well, my car broke down in the desert, and I didn't have the time or the money
14 to fix it, so I sold it.

15 **NANCY** What a shame . . . That was the car your father bought you, wasn't it? But at least
16 you made it. Now let's go home.

17 **REBECCA** That sounds good.

18 **NANCY** Now, where are your bags?

19 **REBECCA** Uh, they're over there. (*The two women turn and look at the bus.*)

20 *The bus driver is unloading the bags. There is a big pile of bags on the ramp.*

21 **NANCY** Are all those yours? . . . Good grief! (*She looks at Rebecca.*) I don't know where we'll
22 put them. Well, we'll figure something out.

23 **REBECCA**   Do they have baggage carts here?

24 **NANCY**   Yes . . . I'll watch your luggage. Why don't you go in and get a cart?

25 *Rebecca pushes a cart full of her baggage to Nancy's car. It is a large old American sedan.*

26 **REBECCA**   I fit all the luggage on the cart, but I can barely see you!

27 **NANCY**   Oh, this way, I got the trunk ready.

28 *Rebecca pushes the cart. Nancy opens the trunk and the back door.*

29 **REBECCA**   Wow, this is quite a car.

30 **NANCY**   It's old, but it runs . . . just like me . . . Here we are . . .

31 **REBECCA**   Be careful. This is heavy.

32 **NANCY**   I'll help do this . . . all right, OK.

33 *Rebecca loads the trunk of the car. Nancy helps with the smaller pieces.*

34 *INSIDE NANCY'S CAR*

35 *Nancy and Rebecca drive through San Francisco.*

36 **REBECCA**   It's hard to believe I'm really in San Francisco.

37 **NANCY**   Well, you are. See that building? That's the TransAmerica building. Some people
38   like it, but not me. It's too big. (*Rebecca looks at the city.*) How's your father?

39 **REBECCA**   He's doing pretty well. His leg bothers him every now and then . . .

40 **NANCY**   I'm sorry to hear that. And your little brother? How's he doing?

41 **REBECCA**   Kevin? He's not so little anymore. He's almost six feet tall, and he just graduated
42   from high school.

43 **NANCY**   Is he going to college?

44 **REBECCA**   At the moment he has a job, but I hope he'll consider it.

45 **NANCY**   A college education is so important these days. It's hard to find a decent job
46   without it.

47 **REBECCA**   You're telling me.

48 **NANCY**   The house isn't very far from here. I hope you'll feel comfortable there.

49 **REBECCA**   I'm sure I will.

50 *Nancy's car pulls onto a quiet street. Rebecca gets out of the car. When she looks up at the house, she is*
51 *surprised at its size. It is a beautiful old Victorian-style home. Nancy and Rebecca stand in front of the*
52 *house.*

53 **REBECCA**   What a beautiful house!

54 **NANCY**   It's been in the family for generations and we love it, but it costs a fortune to
55   keep up.

56 *Nancy takes several small bags and heads toward the house.*

57 **NANCY**   I've got these bags. You get those.

58 *We see Rebecca's face looking up at the house. Then she carries as much of the luggage as she can.*
59 *Rebecca climbs the stairs. Nancy holds the front door open for her. She steps in, sets the bags down, and*
60 *looks around.*

61 **NANCY**   Put those bags down there.

62 **REBECCA**   Oh . . . this house is really a jewel. I see why you've kept it.

63 **NANCY**   Yes . . . it's very special to me. Make yourself at home. It's your home now, too . . .
64   Oh, by the way, there's no smoking and no drugs in the house. And no guests
65   upstairs.

66 **REBECCA**   I don't think you have to worry about that.

67 **NANCY**   I didn't think so.

PART 2

68 *LIBRARY OF NANCY'S HOUSE*

69 *The two women enter and find Melaku, an Ethiopian graduate student, who is studying at a desk.*

70 **NANCY**   Melaku . . . sorry to disturb you. I'd like you to meet my goddaughter.

71 *Melaku removes his glasses, puts aside his books, and stands.*

72 **MELAKU**   Yes, of course, Miss Shaw.

73 **NANCY**   Rebecca Casey, this is Melaku Tadesse.

74 *Rebecca is surprised that another person is in the house.*

75 **MELAKU**   Rebecca? Am I pronouncing your name right? It's a pleasure to meet you.

76 **REBECCA**   Uh . . . It's nice to meet you. Is it Melaku?

77 **MELAKU**   Yes. (*Melaku nods and smiles at Rebecca's pronunciation.*)

78 **NANCY**   Melaku is from Ethiopia. He's a graduate student in business administration.
79   When he gets his degree next year, he'll return home to his wife and two children
80   and start a business in Addis Ababa.

81 **MELAKU**   That is correct . . . Addis Ababa.

82 **REBECCA**   Oh . . .

83 **NANCY**   Rebecca will be studying at the San Francisco College of Music.

84 **MELAKU**   Well, very good. Perhaps you will play or sing for us . . . What do you think, Miss
85   Shaw?

86 **NANCY**   As long as it's not that loud rock music.

87 **REBECCA**   Oh no, don't worry. All I have is an acoustic guitar.

88 **NANCY**   We'll leave you to your studies now.

89 **MELAKU**   I hope you enjoy it here. I do. I'll see you at dinner.

90 **REBECCA**   Thank you. (*They leave and go into the living room.*)

91 *INSIDE THE LIVING ROOM*

92 *Nancy shows Rebecca the living room. Edward Shaw is sitting in a large comfortable chair reading. He*
93 *doesn't realize that they are there.*

94 **NANCY**   This is the living room. My uncle's favorite place. Let me introduce you. Uncle
95   Edward, this is Rebecca Casey, Margaret's daughter.

96 *Mr. Shaw tries to get up. He suffers from arthritis. Nancy helps him.*

97 **NANCY**   Here, let me help you.

98 **REBECCA**   Please, don't trouble yourself.

99 *He smiles at Rebecca and offers his hand.*

100 **EDWARD**   No trouble at all, Rebecca. It's a pleasure to meet you.

101 **REBECCA**   It's very nice to meet you, Mr. Shaw.

102 **EDWARD**   Please call me Edward. I met your mother once, many years ago. You look like
103   her, if memory serves me.

104 **REBECCA**   That's what people tell me . . . I'm very happy to be here.

105 **EDWARD**   We're very glad to have you here. I, uh . . . I think I'd better sit down.

106 *Nancy helps him into his chair.*

107 **EDWARD**   I'm afraid these visits here are rather tiring . . . They take the wind out of
108   my sails.

109 **NANCY**   Can I get you anything?

110 **EDWARD**   No, I'll be fine. Just let me rest a while.

111 **NANCY**   Are you going to stay for supper?

112 **EDWARD**   I wouldn't miss it. Go on now, and show her the rest of the house. And I'll see
113   you at supper, Rebecca.

114 **REBECCA**   That'll be very nice.

115 *Nancy looks at him and then leads Rebecca toward the library. Nancy stops Rebecca and talks quietly to her*
116 *about her uncle.*

117 **NANCY**   My uncle Edward lived in the house his whole life. But his physical condition
118   deteriorated too much, and I had to move him to one of those retirement homes
119   for the elderly. It was a very difficult decision for both of us . . . but at least he
120   comes home once a week. Today's the day.

121 **REBECCA**   He's a very distinguished gentleman.

122 **NANCY**   And he was a very good musician, too . . . He used to play the piano beautifully . . .
123   but he can't anymore . . . He's just too frail . . . Let's see the kitchen.

124 *KITCHEN*

125 **NANCY**   And this is the kitchen . . . *(noticing some crumbs)* Who left this mess? . . . We each
126   buy our own food. *(She opens the refrigerator and kitchen cabinets as she talks.)* We all
127   share the refrigerator, so please put your name on your food. See, like Melaku
128   does.

129 **REBECCA**   Excuse me . . . Does Melaku live here?

130 **NANCY**   Oh, yes. He's one of my renters. He is going to go far, that young man. He's
131   always studying.

132 *Rebecca is starting to realize what this house is—a boarding house. Rebecca, a little surprised, follows*
133 *Nancy. We see containers of food with names on them—Nancy, Melaku, Angela.*

134 **NANCY**   The pots and pans are up here . . . the glasses are here . . . the dishes are here . . .
135   and the utensils are in this drawer. Now . . . you must be thirsty. Would you like
136   some iced tea?

137 REBECCA   Yes, I'd love some, please.

138 *Rebecca sits at the table, quite surprised by the people she has met. Nancy pours her some iced tea.*

139 NANCY   This is the house phone. Local calls are free, but don't stay on too long. Of
140   course, we each pay for our own long-distance calls. We keep a list.

141 *Nancy shows Rebecca the list. The two women sit across from each other.*

142 REBECCA   I . . . didn't know that you had renters.

143 *Nancy realizes she has not yet told Rebecca of her need to take in renters.*

144 NANCY   I didn't write to you about the renters? Oh, Rebecca . . . I'm sorry . . . I'm so
145   embarrassed. I guess I'm not quite used to the idea myself.

146 REBECCA   It was just . . . kind of a surprise.

147 NANCY   Yes, of course. Ever since my uncle moved to the retirement home, the bills have
148   been coming in so quickly. I had to do something. Renting out rooms seemed like
149   a good solution.

150 REBECCA   I'm sure the rent money helps.

151 NANCY   I just couldn't take care of Edward by myself any longer—to bathe him, dress
152   him. And he fell down once when I was out and he couldn't get up by himself . . .
153   It was terrible.

154 REBECCA   I can see it's a big responsibility . . . the house, your uncle . . .

155 NANCY   What choice do I have? (*She shrugs.*) Would you like to see your room?

156 REBECCA   (*smiling*) Yeah.

PART 3

157 *NANCY'S HOUSE, STAIRCASE*

158 *Nancy and Rebecca reach the stairs. Rebecca starts to pick up her bags. Melaku is going to the library.*

159 MELAKU   Oh, please . . . let me help you with those.

160 REBECCA   Oh, thank you. (*He takes several of the suitcases. Nancy also grabs a small bag.*)

161 NANCY   Rebecca, you have enough baggage for an army!

162 REBECCA   I didn't know what I'd need so I brought everything.

163 NANCY   I'm the same way—better safe than sorry.

164 *Melaku follows the two women up to the second floor. Melaku puts down his load and heads up to*
165 *the third floor.*

166 NANCY   Melaku . . . would you put the suitcases in Rebecca's room, please?

167 MELAKU   Of course, Miss Shaw.

168 REBECCA   Thank you. (*She smiles and he nods and heads upstairs.*)

169 NANCY   Melaku lives on the third floor; you and Angela are on the second.

170 REBECCA   Angela?

171 NANCY   Mm-hm.

172 *A bedroom door opens, and Angela appears. She's wearing her bathrobe, heading toward the bathroom.*

173 ANGELA   Oh, hi.

174 **NANCY**   Angela, this is Rebecca Casey, from Boston. She'll be living here, too.

175 **REBECCA**   Hello.

176 **ANGELA**   Oh, terrific! I understand you've had quite an adventure!

177 **REBECCA**   Yes, I . . .

178 **ANGELA**   Is it true you drove all the way across the country by yourself?

179 **REBECCA**   I drove almost all the way.

180 **ANGELA**   Oh, unbelievable! Well, I'm afraid I have to rush. It's nice to meet you. I'll see
181   you later.

182 **REBECCA**   Yes . . . see you later. (*Angela disappears into the bathroom.*)

183 **NANCY**   She's studying to be a nurse, and working part-time. She's kind of wild . . . Well,
184   here we are . . . This is your room.

185 *BEDROOM*

186 *Nancy opens the door to Rebecca's room. Rebecca follows her. The room is small but has plenty of light.*

187 **NANCY**   It's a little dusty . . .

188 **REBECCA**   Oh, it'll be fine . . . It's very charming. (*She takes a look out the window.*) Oh, what a
189   nice view . . . The bed looks comfortable.

190 *Rebecca places her bags on the floor. Nancy sits on the bed to rest and catch her breath. She pats the bed,*
191 *and Rebecca joins her. It is hard for Nancy to tell Rebecca the following news.*

192 **NANCY**   Rebecca, can we talk? (*Rebecca looks at Nancy.*) This is very difficult for me to
193   say . . . You know, I wanted to let you stay here rent-free . . .

194 **REBECCA**   Yes . . . I appreciate that . . .

195 **NANCY**   No, please . . . listen. This is extremely difficult for me. I'm afraid . . . I'll need to
196   ask you for some rent money, to help pay the house expenses.

197 *Rebecca tries to hide her own worry about money.*

198 **NANCY**   I feel bad about this. I've tried everything . . . but if I can't pay my bills, I'll have
199   to sell the house.

200 **REBECCA**   That would be terrible.

201 **NANCY**   The cost of the retirement home is unbelievable . . . much more than we
202   expected.

203 **REBECCA**   I understand . . .

204 **NANCY**   I wish I could help you a little more . . . I mean you are my goddaughter, for
205   heaven's sake!

206 **REBECCA**   I understand. I wanna pay my share. I wanna contribute. How much are you
207   thinking of?

208 **NANCY**   Can you manage two hundred fifty a month?

209 *Rebecca nods. She is thinking about paying all that rent.*

210 **NANCY**   Tell me if you can't afford that much.

211 **REBECCA**   No, it'll be fine . . . two hundred and fifty dollars . . .

212 **NANCY**   Are you sure?

213 **REBECCA**   I'm sure.

214 **NANCY**   It's good to have you here . . . Well, why don't you wash up and settle in a bit?
215   Dinner's at six.

216 **REBECCA**   OK.

217 *Nancy leaves and Rebecca sits and thinks. She is exhausted and a bit surprised by all she has just learned.*